Lazy at Stanford

By Michael Lazaar

DORRANCE PUBLISHING CO
EST. 1920
PITTSBURGH, PENNSYLVANIA 15238

Dorrance Publishing Co
585 Alpha Drive
Pittsburgh, PA 15238
Visit our website at *www.dorrancebookstore.com*

ISBN: 979-8-89027-368-0
eISBN: 979-8-89027-866-1

Lazy at Stanford

Table of Contents

This book is like a Jackson Pollock.

The writing of this book has been both an enjoyable and a learning experience for me. From my experience, I would encourage you to write, for the sheer pleasure, for stimulating thought, as well as for learning about yourself.

I'm aware of the phenomena described in this book in myself. The uncertainty is to what extent are they present in you. I certainly don't claim that the phenomena occur in the entire, or even most, of the population, but if you see yourself in some of what is written here, it could be much to your advantage. Everyone has some of them, to a varying degree.

Although I have done much reading on the subjects presented in this book, this is not intended to be a work of research, nor entirely based on commonly held opinion. It is the product of my own thoughts over the decades, based on years of experience both in relevant settings as well as academic environments.

Sections of this book may be irrelevant to you. You might disagree with parts of it. You might find other parts interesting and valuable. Skip around. Hopefully you will find it stimulating.

*The tall Texan walked into my room
during my freshman year at Stanford.
He saw me staring at my bookshelf.
He said, "I'm going to call you 'Lazy.'"*

This is a book of contradictions.

There is no doubt that not receiving my Stanford degree has had an immensely significant impact on my life. Many times, it seems as if it is the most "traumatic" element of my life, though that is doubtful due to aspects of my childhood.

One of the strongest words of advice I could give anyone, most especially those in elite schools, is to remain in school to get your degree, or else you might spend the rest of your life regretting it. These words are not to be taken lightly. The advantages of having a Stanford degree in our society are enormous. Not only in terms of career advancement, not only in terms of status, but in terms of personal satisfaction as well.

For many reasons, such as the increasing stature of the Stanford degree, the school's emphasis on computer science (my eventual major) and the influence on/location relative to Silicon Valley, the permanence of the name, all the reasons listed below, and most of all, my emotional attachment to the school, not having earned the Stanford degree has simply created a disconcerting issue for me.

The following are reasons why Stanford has been particularly such a thorn in my side:

- It's Rise to #1-2 prominence
- All the *U.S. News and World Report* polls
  - In everything from school, departments, graduate schools, beauty of campus
- See the name so much in the press
- Number of Nobel Laureates
- All the Really Smart People there
- 18 Interdisciplinary Laboratories, Centers, and Institutes
  - Freeman Spogli Institute for International Studies at Stanford

– Center for Advanced Study in the Behavioral Sciences
• (106) Research Centers
  – SAIL (Stanford Artificial Intelligence Laboratory)
  – SLAC National Accelerator Laboratory
  – Hoover Institution
• Psychology (my original perspective major) is perpetually undisputed #1
• Computer Science perpetually undisputed tied for #1
• It's incredible strength in artificial intelligence, a dream field of mine
• Silicon Valley
  – Spawned by Stanford
  – Home of my field, the computer field
  – Current huge societal emphasis on Silicon Valley
  – Big-name tech companies/start-ups in Palo Alto
• California/Bay Area beauty
• San Francisco – What I believe to be the most beautiful city in U.S. is 45 minutes away
• The weather
• Beauty of campus
• The phenomenon of the campus
  – Rodin Sculpture Garden
  – Golf Course – Robert Trent Jones designed
  – Quad / Palm Drive
  – Spectacular Faculty Housing
  – Frank Lloyd Wright House
  – Architecture – The Quad, housing clusters, Old Union, The Claw
  – Stanford Research Park – World's First University Research Park
  – The largest contiguous campus in the U.S.
• Wealth/houses of area
• Sand Hill Road Venture Capitalists
• Money – All about getting rich – the endowment is currently 4th
• Funkiness
• The Band
• Sports
  – Outstanding Athletic Program – Currently has Won the Directors Cup 25 Years in a Row for the Most Success in College Athletics

- Most NCAA Division I Team Championships
- Most NCAA Division I Team and Individual Championships
- Great programs compared to other Top Academic schools [Ivy League]
- Great Football Tradition – Pop Warner
- Football – 4 BCS bowls in a row last decade. Rose Bowl 3 out of 4 years in a row
- Basketball – ranked #1 several years in a row
- Sports facilities – Stadium, Maples, sunken diamond, aquatic complex, tennis complex

• California/San Francisco culture, as in what they're into (at least back then), such as developing consciousness.

• Social Consciousness of Students and University

• Palo Alto – one of the most desirable towns to live in.

• How the school pushes its name. For example, in 1984-85, they hosted both Olympic events and the Super Bowl.

• The Entire Undergraduate Experience

Society's "newfound" emphasis on getting into "elite" schools has also played an enormous role in my enormous issue of not having received my Stanford degree. The much-heightened emphasis seemed to have started in the 80s, possibly late 80s. It became do-or-die for children, especially children of the upper-middle-class (I hate to use the concept of class, but it does fit here) to get accepted into an elite school. The book, *Excellent Sheep,* talks about this in great detail. This emphasis greatly highlighted the "name" of a school/university, which added much more significance to the name "Stanford" and therefore having it on your degree.

There were also familial pressures from my childhood. My parents, both intelligent people, placed an enormous value on education. There were socio-economic and cultural family pressures as well. One year, in eighth grade, I brought home all As and a B. My mother said, "(I'd like to see you) turn that B into an A."

In my family, I had an absolutely horrible relationship with my brother. In our sibling rivalry, my getting good grades was "my way of getting the upper hand" on him. The emphasis on education in my family facilitated my being able to use education and grades as a "weapon" towards him and was one of the main roots of my resultant educational emphasis, and therefore the extreme valuing of a Stanford degree.

There is no doubt my abundance of respect for the school has made me want the degree just to have it, and also for my belief in how much further I would have gone with it. I feel/think very close to the school and always have since the moment I was accepted. I would say abnormally close. Could I have gotten this way, could I have thought about it this much, if it were avoidant to me? Avoidant, as in a negative stimulus, something to keep away from.

However, I really wonder how people who have earned the degree really feel about having attained the degree. Do they walk around in a state of bliss? Or do they also have complexes, such as, in some cases, not having gone on to a top-tier graduate school? Or having graduated from both Stanford and a top-tier graduate school, but then not having gone on to an extremely successful career? Or, not having reached the absolute pinnacle of their chosen field?

Had bipolar disorder not manifested itself while at Stanford, at the age of 19, which is an extremely if not statistically the most common age for the disorder to appear, I most likely would have remained, graduated, and moved on. Also, I became very selective in what classes I attended and in what readings I chose. This caused my grades to veer from the near straight As that it takes to get into Stanford, toward a less desirable state.

I have realized, in my being so obsessed with Stanford, that the name of a school means something, possibly a lot, but not super-much. Your education, where you went to school, *does* mean a lot in our society. But I believe I over-emphasize it.

For example, the girl at the dinner party drops the name of <u>where she went to school</u>. But it does not dominate the conversation. People don't *all* wear shirts with the name in huge lettering. It is on the resume, but so are other things. And it's at the bottom. And when a company sends out an announcement about a new hire, or a promotion, they mention what school(s) the person attended, but again, it is at the bottom. Or when Forbes or a similar publication lists the world's billionaires and give a three-line bio next to their name, they also list the name of the person's school, but again usually at the bottom. But they do list it. These orthodox listings further accentuate my issue of not having attained my Stanford degree.

This "partial meaning" could lead to selective reinforcement, meaning that once you add credence to it, it only takes a certain number of subsequent exposures to continue your belief that, in this case, the name of your school is dispro-portionately large.

When I thought of all the people I had learned anything from, the first person who popped into my head, came into my mind, was Daryl Bem, my Psychology 1 Professor freshman year at Stanford in the fall quarter. I felt a split-second, huge rush. Does this imply that I received, extracted so much more from my Stanford education (than most people, due to the magnitude of the rush) than I have led myself to believe? Does the lack of attainment of the S.U. degree make me believe that I extracted next to nothing out of my Stanford education? (There is a societal reinforcement for no degree that you are not as smart as someone who received one, in this case having received one from the same school.) And just as much, does it prevent me from believing/*accepting* that I received an exceptional amount out of my Stanford education?

Why does this matter *so* much to me? Why do I take the university so seriously? *Is it a sign of high (advanced) intelligence?*

The Stanford choice to follow my own intellectual "journey" may have very well been a superior choice to the path of pursuing As.

Bipolar Disorder

Bipolar disorder is an "illness" of energy. Or, better said, it's best, most accurately seen as a *phenomenon* of energy.

A burst of good news, which can excite someone, can lead to sensations of mania.

At the very end of the day, when most people get tired, some people get depressed (low mood) because tired equals low energy.

In the sections of this work where I discuss bipolar disorder, I focus on the manic side.

It is important for me to state that I am not academically trained in bipolar disorder. My knowledge and statements on the condition are derived from years of reading on the subject, including significant portions of the authoritative text on the subject: *Manic-Depressive Illness: Bipolar Disorder and Recurrent Depression*. Other significant sources over the years include therapy and therefore rich discussions with highly trained clinicians, and the many notes taken from the sessions. Also contributing is having studied psychology at Stanford, as well as intensive thought from an active mind.

The Manic Door

A phenomenon I have consistently experienced is what I call the "manic door." It occurs when a series of rational thoughts escalate my thinking process, taking me into a low level of mania, perhaps best described as a hypomanic state. (Hypomania is a less intense form of mania, usually absent of delusional thinking, but still characterized by an escalated, sped-up thought process). The escalating thoughts that lead me through the manic door are characterized by a higher-than-normal level of intelligence. An intelligent thought leads to a more intelligent thought, which continues to spiral upward until the manic threshold is reached.

It is intuitively obvious, through an honest process of self-observation, that it is the cognitive thought-chain that is leading me up in energy, as opposed to primarily a biological event. Obviously, there is an associated neurological, biological phenomenon that parallels this escalating event, but it is clear to me, through my experience, that the thoughts, the cognitive element, take precedence in the causality in the escalation. A neuroscientific perspective would say that the event is caused by a biological phenomenon, and the thought-train is simply a by-product of the biological event. Also, there are theories that claim that a person is unable to correctly observe their cognitive states, i.e., that this "cognitive escalation" is in fact an illusion and is strictly biologically driven. It is only through my direct observation that I see the manic door, using the same facilities of perception that I use in everyday perception of cognitive phenomena such as language, etc.

Current theory would state that there is a biological predisposition to mania. And that a "normal" person, someone without bipolar disorder, could and would experience intelligent, if not very intelligent, thoughts without entering a hypomanic state. Granted. And let's assume I most likely have a biological predisposition to mania. And that it is this biological predisposition to mania that is "triggered" by the intelligent thought-chain. However, a main point is that the thought-to-hypomania event is *initiated* by the thoughts, by the cognitive event, as opposed to simply the biological mania "turning on" by itself.

You can take the biological reductionist model where all cognitive events, all events of will, are "simply" biological, neurological events, and are *best* seen that way. But at some point, you have to compartmentalize thought, you have to point to something, some subset of neurological processes, and call that "thought." And it is that thing, thought, that *leads* the mind/brain into the hypomanic state, in a *smooth* fashion, not necessarily linear, but along a smooth curve as if having a will of its own and *guiding* the escalation process. And that the thoughts are headed in that direction before any mania or biological process kicks in.

You can take the explanation that even the initial thought is driven by mania. But then you've got to say that *every thought I have* is driven by my bipolar disorder. This robs me of the ability to produce rational thought. Which I know I am capable of doing. Further, according to your logic, everything about me can be seen to be a manifestation of bipolar disorder. I believe this is drastically pathologizing the condition and taking away everything else that I am.

Further, it has been said that there is a correlation between intelligence and creativity, and mania. The current explanation is that it is the manic potential which allows for heightened creativity. Perhaps the causality should be looked at in reverse, as is many times the case, in that people who possess higher levels of creativity and intelligence are more likely to experience "being taken" through the manic door.

It would be a shame to pathologize the thought escalation process, which is a gift when experienced and controlled, into an illness.

My whole premise is that the psychological perspective presents a very significant reference frame for viewing and understanding manic episodes. This is evidenced here by how the intelligent, if not very intelligent thoughts, as a cognitive event, are the precipitating factor in entering the manic state. I state that it is the intelligent thoughts that are the primary cause of entering the manic state, with the biological predisposition simply making it possible.

I just received a great compliment on my career and academic accomplishments from a *very* respectable neighbor. It caused me to get very excited. Not quite hypomanic, but toward that state. Once again, my biology enabled the excitement to occur. But it was obviously a cognitive, psychological event, the compliment and its psychological response that caused the excitement.

It is the premise of cognitive therapy that thoughts can influence emotion. Just as "positive thoughts" can reverse a person's negative thoughts, and thereby eradicate a depressed mood, I claim that very intelligent thoughts can influence mood as well.

Intelligence is often seen as an arousing, energetic state. Like that lightbulb turning on in your head.

It should be said here that an overwhelming amount of current scientific evidence holds that bipolar disorder is a biological disorder, caused by both genetic and environmental influences. I am not arguing this. I believe the ratio of genetic predisposition and environmental influence differs by individual, but both apparently must be present for the illness to manifest itself. Three cups of strong coffee can induce a hypomanic state, which shows the influence biology can have. Research will uncover more about which genetic clusters are responsible for a bipolar predisposition, as well as not only the areas of the brain that become affected but the specific neurological events that occur during a manic episode. It has even been said that bipolar disorder is a biological event masquerading as a psychological one. I strongly believe, however, and I hope it is apparent here, that a manic event also has powerful psychological properties, that the psychological dynamics are being minimized in favor of the current strides in genetic and neurological research, and that the psychological perspective presents a unique and extremely insightful perspective for understanding the disorder.

Medical Doctor's Biological Bias

Medical Doctors are saints. I say that to the fullest extent of my mind and heart. They sacrifice decades in order to study and train intensively. Their subjects are difficult, and they must achieve very high grades. Their training does not end with school; their residencies require long hours and even more years. This is all undergone in order to dedicate themselves to serve people in their time of need. The following is not at all meant to be "critical," but hopefully to help establish my point.

Historically, the basis of a doctor's education is in the biological sciences. The most common, favored major to be accepted into medical school is biology, or a derivative of it, such as microbiology. Therefore, they have a biological versus an environmental orientation.

This, certainly as explained by medical history, is due to the simple, obvious fact that doctors have focused on the person's body when treating the sick person. Body equals biology. It is this biological bias, I believe, that prevents modern psychiatry from looking at bipolar disorder, and possibly other emotional illnesses significantly from the psychological perspective. Also, research conducted by the medical community tends to focus on the biological aspect of the illness. Granted, of course, that biology plays a very significant role in many emotional illnesses, but it is my belief, based on my self-observation and personal experiences, that the psychological perspective is also very significant.

Granted, genetics play a very significant role in bipolar disorder, and much progress has been made in recent years on the relationship of genetics to bipolar disorder. But it is precisely because of this progress, and focus of research, that it seems like everyone has "hopped on the genetic bandwagon" to the point of minimizing, and losing sight of, the past and present environmental and situational causes, as well as the accompanying psychological phenomena.

Biological reductionism – the act of studying cognitive phenomena and emotional illness primarily as a biological, as opposed to psychological event, is a prevalent scientific perspective today. However, I believe the biological perspective "reduces" the emotional illness to a physical phenomenon as opposed to also a very revealing, psychological experience.

I am not taking the point of view that the mind exists separate from the body, nor am I saying it doesn't, but the mind is certainly a powerful entity in and of itself and should at least in one perspective be looked upon as a whole, complete entity.

I do believe in the power and incredible usefulness of medication to treat bipolar disorder as well as other emotional maladies. Just because a condition may also be psychological in nature does not mean that it cannot be approached strictly biologically. The mind and brain are heavily linked and treating one with the other is entirely possible. Therapy can influence biological states just as medication can influence psychological ones. Severe cases, in fact, in some instances can only initially be treated pharmaceutically; the miracle is that they can then be "brought down" to the point where therapists can take over, in conjunction with continued use of medication.

People constantly look for a biological attribution to their state: for example, someone not feeling up to par before a final exam might attribute their condition to, "it was something I ate," rather than attributing their nervousness to something in their present environment, namely taking the exam.

The attribution of "it was something I ate" is an extremely common one, providing a convenient "scapegoat" for psychological events. As another example, "it was something I ate" may also be attributed to a pill or drug more so than the person's psychological state of mind or the (immediate) perception right in front of you.

Ego as Manic Door

As a pointed example of how the ego acted like a manic door in my life, I equate a sharp rise in self-image as an expression and advancement of ego (the extreme of which is "I am great"). One time, I took part in a weight-loss program; I believe it was either Nutri-System or Jenny Craig. On the day that I hit my goal weight, as told so in their center, I went into a manic episode. On that same day, I was taken off lithium completely after being carefully titrated off, down to being told to use it every other day. On a separate occasion, years later, after being enrolled in another instance of a weight-loss program, again I went into a manic episode on the same day as reaching my goal weight. I do believe that the act of hitting my goal weight greatly boosted my self-image, and therefore expressed and advanced my ego, and once again launched me into a manic episode. The question for you is: did I associate the attainment of the goal weight with being taken off lithium, and therefore the removal of lithium was the cause of my entering a manic episode the first time, and that I went into a manic episode "by association" in the later episode when the weight loss occurred, but lithium wasn't involved?

If, though, you support the belief system that environmental factors are a very significant component of manic episodes, then this goes a long way toward providing evidence that the psychological is a powerful determinant in triggering a manic episode.

Entering mania, through the manic door or otherwise, is seen as a consequence of behavior, of thought, or of perception, as opposed to strictly a biological event.

People with bipolar disorder are held to a narrower range of everything when in fact they have a wider than "normal" but still within "normal" non-pathological bounds. This applies to people with bipolar disorder who are under control.

A manic person with expanded range is, after diagnosis, restricted to a more (sometimes much more) narrow (than normal) range of behavior (i.e., can't wake up early or sleep late). A DSM symptom of bipolar disorder is "decreased need for sleep," and I'm sure, like in "decreased appetite" as a symptom and "increased appetite" as a symptom, you will be able to find "increased need for sleep." You will find that people with bipolar disorder will vary more than people without the disorder.

Once again there is an "average" range, a "wide but normal" range, and a pathological range. People with bipolar disorder in the wide but normal range are forced not only into the average range, which pathologizes any behavior outside of the average range, but often to tighter bounds inside the normal range. This obviously creates difficulties for people with bipolar disorder who are simply behaving within a normal accepted range.

I thought of something that made me smile. *Oh my GOD...*

> Modeling: what if some symptoms are "learned behaviors":
> 1. Due to a person's tendency, they have a more varied need for sleep. Then say that person gets up with a lot less sleep two nights in a row (which is completely normal),
> 2. Is told, "You are manic," and 2a. believes it due to the source,
> 3. Then looks to model someone with bipolar disorder. He/she has knowledge of what the symptoms of bipolar disorder are and then incorporates them into his behavior.
> 4. He/she then self-perceives their symptoms and becomes much more convinced that he/she has bipolar disorder. Then he/she has entered the vicious cycle of:
>   a. belief of perception,
>   b. modeling someone with bipolar disorder,
>   c. believing the bipolar disorder self-perception that much further, and
>   d. more modeling, etc.

Obviously, a person could not go into a full-blown manic episode, nor develop bipolar disorder simply by modeling people who have it. But I wonder to what extent symptoms could be manufactured.

The vicious cycle eventually winds down, possibly due to the fact that the original and subsequent perceptions are not strong enough to hold up against other, more "normal" perceptions from reality.

Here, bipolar disorder and other illnesses might be seen to have a component of being a "learned behavior." They apply the narrow range to themselves and, when applying self-perception, become convinced that they are in more of a state of the illness than they are.

Of course, the bipolar disorder occurs for accepted reasons, i.e., genetic, biological, and environmental. I am merely suggesting there may be a "learned behavior" aspect to symptoms as well.

The Common Cold

As an aside, the common cold has always mystified me. How come whenever I think about it, I feel cold symptoms? The common cold is no doubt viral in nature. Also, a person can catch a cold simply by being "cold," presumably, according to modern science, if the virus is present in the person. But is it possible that symptoms are also spread through the mechanism of social learning? In other words, the observation of someone with a cold can lead to someone developing cold symptoms themselves. I am not suggesting that colds don't spread due to the spreading of virus germs. But perhaps there is something more taking place. A social learning/observation aspect would help explain the "contagious" aspect of colds, as well as the spreading of viral germs do.

If this is the case, I believe there is an "empathy" factor in determining a person's susceptibility to "learning" a cold. The higher a degree of empathy a person's personality has, the more likely they are to "feel" someone else's biological state, and perhaps "feel" that person's cold symptoms.

An interesting psychology experiment would be to place a healthy subject in a room and show them a video of someone who has a cold. That way, cold symptoms are observed without the germ contact. Then see if the subject develops any cold symptoms. Or in fact a full-blown cold. A full-blown cold would be unlikely through observation alone, without the presence of a cold virus. Probably only symptoms, short-lived, could occur this way. As a control group, you would need subjects in the same room exposed to the same person on a similar video, but healthy.

What if symptoms are spread through observation, or other means such as reading or word of mouth, through social learning? What would be the ramifications? What would be the evolutionary advantages? A keener awareness of someone else's illness in order to help that person get better?

What if people have developed different ranges of emotion, as in different extensions of the emotional spectrum, and only occasionally they have an aberration, or blip, on their "higher," "more intense," or what you would call "manic" side. An observer who does not experience such extensions and observes this temporary blip in the intense side of the scale, might be quite likely to label it as "mania." The point being that the extension of the emotional spectrum should not be seen as being pathological, especially in light of the fact that the blip, or abnormal behavior, is very rare.

The Effect of Nuvigil and the Cognitive Pressure Theory of Mania
One of many theories I have on bipolar disorder is the pressure cooker concept. It is related to my homeostasis belief of the human mind and body.

The theory relates to two experiences I have had related to medication I have taken for bipolar disorder. In the first instance, I was somewhat heavily medicated. This caused a "downward push" on my cognitive states. The interesting effect is that, instead of staying "down," I actually swung the other way, into a manic state sooner than usual in my manic pattern. I believe this was due to me swinging up from the downward-pressured state, into a higher-than- "normal" state (the manic state), due to the force of homeostasis. I believe homeostasis, or the cycling of the body and perhaps mind back to a "normal" state, is a powerful force, and perhaps parts of medicine should be more geared toward letting, and encouraging, the body's force of homeostasis take over and let the body heal itself.

The second experience involved Nuvigil. Nuvigil is a medication which is approved for wakefulness but is also used to combat the dulling effects of some medications. What Nuvigil does for me is elevate my cognitive level, bringing me closer to, but not into, a manic state.

Intuitively thinking, one would think that Nuvigil would "cause" one to enter mania on a recurrent basis. But the interesting effect that Nuvigil had on me is that I have not had a manic episode since being placed on Nuvigil. I strongly believe that this is due to the fact that Nuvigil "took the pressure cooker" pressure off and let me exist much closer to my natural state within my natural range. Because I was closer to my "higher" at times somewhat hypomanic state, but not over it, there was much, much less of a homeostatic force pushing me up and over into mania.

I also had a particularly very positive experience on Nuvigil. Having been started on Nuvigil right before a huge SAN support issue (a SAN, or Storage Area Network, is an extremely complex system of computer technology. It connects many computers, some very large, using fiber optic connections, to in this case extremely large "arrays," or cabinets, of disk drives, in a major corporate datacenter. The amount of data on the disk arrays totals into the multiple petabyte scale, or simply put, a lot of Wikipedia's.).

It was my turn on the support cycle, so I led the support effort. There were approximately 50 people involved from three different companies.

The "project" turned out to be extremely successful. All the aspects were remediated. "Root cause," or finding the initial causes of all ten issues, were found. I received a lot of recognition from management, including a significant bump up in my annual review.

Nuvigil absolutely played a role in this. I would take my Nuvigil in the morning, then have my iced teas at the beginning of the 50-person conference calls which I led. I had confidence and strength of leadership.

This is yet one more experience where a substance can enhance performance, let alone work performance.

It should be noted that there are warnings attached to the use of Nuvigil for people who have experienced mania and other psychological disorders. Though my doctor, who is very experienced and extremely well-qualified, has not observed any issues with it, a person should still consult with their doctor before using Nuvigil.

For me, every major, or even just significant, decision, seems to pass through a "filter" of, "Am I manic?" as if I am incapable of making a decision while in a supposed manic state. This implies that mania, to any degree, causes a complete shutdown of my rationality, which it does not. In fact, it has been written that mild mania sharpens the mind and associated cognitive faculties.

In fact, simply making a significant decision "triggers," not only the "manic check," but erroneously makes me believe that the decision came from the mania-caused irrational state.

Causes of My Bipolar Disorder
- Genetic – created genetic predisposition.
- Past history – environmental horrible brother.

- *Lost grades*. Both cause and effect.
  - Grades and all that is academic superiority, except the fact that I was at Stanford which gave me a sense of academic superiority. There was an emotional up-and-down motion of mania-lost grades-mania-etc., which further could have triggered the disorder.
  - Stopped doing some homework/going to some classes.
- Lost track/sports
- Lost car (great car)
- Pot
  - Played an unspecified role in losing grades.
  - Too intellectually stimulating.
- *Onset of adult life*, key life turning point. Career, future, *need to make a living.*
  - *The removal of the security of living at home with <u>subsistence</u> all taken care of by parents, and the subsequent need to "go out in the world" and make a living. "Leaving the nest."*
  - Grades played *huge* role in future career. Effect of loss of grades was amplified by advent of need to make a living.
- Being placed into a new social environment.
- Detachment from society and/or people – both cause and effect.
- Environment of being at Stanford – "being high up societal scale."
- Some sort of intelligence, capacity of mind.
- Another huge determinant: 1) <u>Liberal</u> school; 2) Bay Area (extremely, most liberal part of country); 3) early mid-70s, carry over from 60s. The 60s, including the music, *matured* in the early 70s; 4) *very* far away from home, out there by myself; 5) never lived away from home before on a quasi-permanent basis (except summer camp); 6) *a great school that encouraged independent, original, creative, non-conforming thought.*

Superboy Complex: Manic Episodes are Seen in One Sense as a Way to Recapture Past Glory

Superboy Theory: At one time having achieved "glory," then losing it. Having been a *high achiever.*" The mind "recreates" the "high" of the achieved state.

A primary cause of bipolar disorder, at least with me, is the superboy complex.

Having had (childhood) "greatness" or at least high achievement. In my case, mostly grades, but also sports. Then temporarily losing it all. The entering of the manic state can be seen as a way to recapture the past glory.

A parallel case: rock stars (and in fact, anyone in rock and roll who has been in the limelight) recapturing the incredible high, the rush of being on stage in the limelight by using drugs. Which is why drug use, extreme drug use, is extremely prevalent in rock and roll, and to a lesser but still very significant extent in sports, and occupies a very significant place in both their cultures.

In fact, it can be said that one cause of certain types of drug use for a lot of people is to recapture, re-experience moments of glory.

Also, possibly one reason why people with bipolar disorder seek drugs: to recreate the manic high.

Looking at My Parents as Coaches: Is That Healthy?

Coach: Very authoritarian; completely goal oriented. The only role he plays in your life is to get you to win/succeed.

The "sphere" of the parents is so large that is it possible to have "10 percent" of their "purpose" to get you to win/succeed, and this "10 percent" is as large as a coach, i.e., large enough to be referred to as a role of coach. But there is still the other 90%.

How my relationship with beast was congruent with the vertical space between us, i.e., when I was doing very well and he was doing very badly, we did not get along at all; in fact, it was quite vicious.

For example: Childhood. Me, a high A student, and him, C and lower student. Our relationship was horrendous. Then, for a brief period, when he was at R.U., and I was in between university high success, we got along, or at least better than "usual."

Before that and after, like when he came to visit me at R.U. when I was academically succeeding very highly in C.S. and he was on bicycle in the lowest of low places in society, he became very aggressive again in my dorm room. And beyond. This gap might very well have been one of the contributors to his going insane. (Mostly by completely dropping out of society and into the lowest socio-economic rung.)

There's an enormous similarity between coming on in a "manic state" and coming on in "mescaline." Mescaline let me "see" (as in Aldous Huxley's *The Doors of Perception*: he took mescaline, and he was able to "perceive/see"). As in, manic state enables me to see *the truth*.

Or did mescaline create neural pathways of "mania" with or without genetic predisposition. Then, these pathways are (very) easily opened through certain subsequent experiences.

I say: I might have *learned* the manic state from mescaline/pot. The mind experiences a superior/more pleasurable state. It learns that the state is good. Having learned the state, the mind then becomes capable of bringing it on without the outside "stimulus," the catalyst of drugs. My mind induces the manic state to "recapture" the mescaline experience with the genetic predisposition.

This is why possibly over time it takes less and less environmental/circumstantial stimulus to cause the manic state. The mind has learned the state, and each occurrence of mania reinforces the learning, thereby making it easier for the mania to come on again. This would explain the "kindling effect."

A key cause of going manic: A *positive* element of some sort usually, if not must (with me), be present. In fact, I wonder if, with some episodes (not all), a negative element has to be present to trigger a manic episode. There are always negative, stressful elements in a person's life, and therefore, you will find it when looking; however, I wonder if you look for an outstanding, rare and positive event, that you will find that, too. For example, one of my manic episodes was triggered by success with a technologically advanced project; another episode began when a desirable employment opportunity materialized into a large offer.

On Pathologizing the Manic State

When my therapist saw a page in my notebook that contained on it what was essentially one of my major breakthroughs as captured on paper, written excitedly, he basically accused me of having written that page while manic. In fact, when I brought up a topic of how intelligent I at times thought I might be, meaning was I accurate in thinking that I might be quite above-average intelligent, he said to "err on the side of caution."

This shows 1) the impact that being diagnosed with bipolar disorder has on how you are viewed; he thought I am manic when I think I am possibly well-above average intelligence, and 2) the impact on what the therapist says on the patient (I had to wrestle with his statement for quite a while).

The Elastic Band (one more explanation/method of entering the manic state)
When you "come out" of the low state, the normal tendency is to move into the normal state. However, your "*momentum*" takes, pushes you *beyond* the normal state into the very high, manic state.

Call it momentum. Or homeostasis. Also, it can cycle back, especially if the person does not have a well-formed ego (to "catch" and stabilize it). Here, the ego is seen as a solidified self-image that lies between a large, boisterous self-image and a small, inferiority-complex self-image.

Compensation
There is another somewhat related version of the Elastic Band theory. It occurs when the person has a genuine deficiency. In the manic state, the deficient item becomes greatly magnified, becoming a great, very positive attribute. For example, as you probably have read by now, I struggle greatly with the fact that I did not obtain my Stanford degree. When in a normal, non-manic state, I can still think about Stanford in a positive light but am greatly disturbed by the fact that I did not graduate. When I had been in a manic state, Stanford becomes very greatly magnified in a very positive way and occupies one of many very significant parts of my manic experience.

Another good example is this girl I used to know in college. I became quite infatuated with her. In a normal state of mind, I know that there was no romantic relationship there. In my manic states, however, she becomes equally infatuated with me.

There is definitely an element of compensation or escaping/thinking that the inferiority does not exist, in what drives my manic behavior in certain cases.

And that, coupled with 1) being told I am superboy by parents, 2) straight-A's in accelerated classes, 3) Stanford, 4) to a lesser extent track and camp best athlete award, 5) computer field-director raves-good reviews-great compliments from key peers, etc., 6) Rutgers-C.S.-hardest classes-A's in them-Compiler: O.S.: Syntax Directed Editor-Neural Network-Java-Steven's grades-two microcode programs - Finite State Machines: pumping lemma-every program I ever wrote ran; 7) Bell Labs-high rating; The whole mix/complex/"syndrome" can lead in my case to a "Complex of Extreme Superiority" (manic delusion).

However, that still doesn't <u>prove</u> wrong the possibility that there are excellences about me. When I go manic, do I see the truth? Or come close to it (just a bit higher)?

Like excelling in Bell Labs. But what about the fact that many people received '1's on their Bell Labs appraisals? Then what about the creators of UNIX?

The Manic Dilemma

In fact, the above is a very profound element of the manic experience. It is the conflict between 1) are you living in a world where you are not excellent, but exaggerate out of inferiorities and "minor excellences," or 2) genuinely being exceptional, having enough character traits (nice guy, etc.) and personal attributes to genuinely be "high," meaning to justifiably think of yourself in a very "high" way.

That is part of the phenomenon of over-attribution to the manic state, and over-attribution to having bipolar disorder. Such as, believing that so much of your thought and emotions are due to mania, such as the thought of being exceptional in a select few areas.

As another example of over-attribution to the manic state, sometimes I write very expressively. I will use '!' more frequently than most people. This morning when I was making notes to myself, I used one. I said to myself, "I must be feeling manic," or "Oh, that's a reflection of your bipolar." It can get to the point where every uplifting moment and emotion can be labeled as a byproduct of having bipolar disorder. This is a form of pathologizing.

Bipolar Personality

Meaning, bipolar disorder caused by lifetime experiences as well as genetics. For example, acceptance, attending, part of Stanford community, and then leaving without a degree, caused "wave" motion such that each successive reflective experience of it *magnified* the wave of acceptance/Stanford experience (to compensate for loss) but then the "loss emotion" was also magnified due to the drop. The wave's amplitude stretched: the high got higher, and therefore, the low got lower. This caused or at least greatly attributed to a bipolar disorder syndrome/complex in me.

Also caused by life history/experiences. (Somehow) my personal history was more "up and down," such as: bringing home excellent grades versus beast. I've won many awards, yet not won some I should've. I've received a lot of recognition and praise in my career yet have been slighted in serious ways when I shouldn't have been.

Even in track, I was "inconsistent." More good races, some bad. More extremely good, some extremely bad. The primary facet of the bipolar personality: experiencing extreme highs and lows in life independent of having bipolar disorder, thereby feeding the "bipolar syndrome." In other words, the "bipolar life" is seen to be a cause of bipolar disorder, not the other way around. Of course, I'm not saying there is no "natural" bipolar disorder, just that the bipolar personality that develops over time acts to accentuate the disorder.

Along these lines, do certain "life configurations" lend themselves to the manifestation, possibly the severity of bipolar disorder? Such as being on a great basketball team, but not being very good? Or living in a wealthy town, but not having wealth. Or working for a company that is not well-known but being extremely talented and making a huge contribution. These "polarities" would have to be somewhat extreme, and a person would have to have a fair amount of them, as well as a genetic pre-disposition to have any effect on their personality and certainly their bipolar disorder. Or perhaps I just perceive my highs and lows to be higher and lower than the average person because of my disorder.

Cultural Evolutionary Determinants of Bipolar Disorder

Our times may be conducive to the development of bipolar disorder.

The huge polarity of this day and age on a societal scale can be seen to parallel the polarity within an individual. The reality of microprocessors and the internet is on the advanced side of the spectrum, enabling great achievement and entertainment. But we still have wars, poverty, and disease. The outstanding and the horrible. This current state in our cultural evolution could be seen to influence individual states of mind if you are willing to consider the possibility that there is a relationship between disease and society. Where did hysteria, a disease of Freud's day, go? Did it possibly evolve as culture did?

Bipolar illness goes undiagnosed to a great degree. It is also quite possible that, although many people don't have bipolar disorder, they may believe they do, at least at certain times. This could very well be due to the enormous change, the instability of our times, of the past 40 years or so. Not only does the modern era bring cultural swings, but these swings also result in personal swings as well. This should not be pathologized; only a sliver, one percent as it is published, actually have diagnosable bipolar disorder.

On the correlation between smoking pot and subsequent development of mania-related symptoms: first of all, people tend to smoke pot for the first time in their mid-teens, and the established age for the onset of bipolar disorder is 19 or thereabouts, if not 19 then usually later.

I believe that a certain type of personality is attracted to pot, someone who is attracted to beautiful, colorful, artistic tapestries, and the special music of the reefer people. This attraction brings them to try marijuana, and in many (not all, not some) cases, they become "regular" smokers. I believe this same "mindset," this same curiosity, seeking of "higher," richer, more perceptually intense, and more cognitive states, is what leads some of their minds to the manic state.

People with emotional illnesses are by far the most discriminated against group of people. More so than any gender, race, or ethnic group.

Ego Trip (Things Good In, but I Think Are Much Better When Manic)
- Intelligence
- Writing
- Great at technology, money, music, art
- Baby Boomers: Kesey, pot, music, cultural engagement, elite schools/degrees, musical culture (Beatles, Bob D…)
- Computer Science, UNIX, Storage, Windows dexterity, Networking, etc. (I *do* think I am very good in Programming.)

Example: Buying a Car "During a Manic Episode"
I just *think* of buying a car. *Then* I get excited-manic about buying a car. Then I purchase the car, thinking afterwards that I bought the car in a manic state. The true sequence is that you had decided to buy the car first, which caused excitement, then you bought the car. The buying of the car caused the manic state; however, the mania occurred before the purchase due to the excitement of buying one.

Causality: manic, then car? NO.

Car, then manic? YES.

Positive Attributes of My Manic States

There is no doubt a correlation between intelligence and bipolar disorder.

Here, mania is not seen as being strictly pathological but as a "parallel" extension of intelligence. Intelligence is a (energy) heightened state of mind, like mania; like how drinking a cup of coffee perks you up, makes you more "intelligent." Intelligence can then be seen as a heightened state of mind, similar to, but certainly not identical to, mania.

Spouse's Reaction to Manic State

A particularly difficult subject is the issue of the spouse's, or partner's, reaction to someone being in the manic state.

On one hand, it is well-known, by both the field and by the patient, that mania is an illness that occurs involuntarily. Contrary to a misheld belief, the person has no control on the entrance into the manic state. While some of us might enjoy two cups of coffee in the morning, almost no one would voluntarily enter a full-blown manic state. Those of us who have been there are fully aware of the negative consequences, at times devastating, to relationships, to work, possibly financially, and many other undesirable consequences.

Therefore, intuitively, you would think that the spouse or significant other would have total tolerance of someone in the manic state just as one would expect a person not to be angry at someone coming out of remission in cancer or developing a bad illness of another sort. (Note: though bipolar disorder is a serious illness, I have never been comfortable comparing it to cancer. Bipolar disorder is a completely different phenomenon in and of itself, unlike any other illness, and much less fatal. Unlike "strictly" physical illnesses—if any illness is strictly physical—, not only is everyone's experience of bipolar disorder different, but it really has to be experienced to fully comprehend it.)

On the other hand, one must look at how a spouse or partner experiences someone in a manic state. Many times, it is no joy. In fact, it can be quite devastating to see your significant other "turn into someone else." The sharp displays of anger, irritability, and outright hostility that *sometimes*, and I emphasize *sometimes*, accompanies the manic state only adds to the burden of living with someone who is in a manic state.

Some truly undesirable circumstances arise. It is when the manic episode is at its extremes when a spouse might reach out to the manic husband/wife/partner for support, and it is precisely under the conditions produced by a manic partner that produces this need, only to not have the person available for support due to being in a manic state, to "be someone else."

Also, when one is the victim of manic hostility, it is extremely difficult, if not impossible, to contain the reactive emotion of anger back toward the source. A hostile person can be very difficult to live with.

Then there are the worries that the spouse, in a manic state, might engage in very foolish destructive behaviors, financial or otherwise, that might have dire consequences for both partners in the relationship, if not the entire family.

So, while rationally speaking, one would expect and hope that the spouse treats mania strictly as an involuntary illness, emotionally in many circumstances that might not be possible and needs to be understood as such, especially after the manic episode has come to an end.

A huge caveat to this, however, is the actual severity of the manic episode. Many, if not most all, episodes are non-violent, and not typified by outbursts of anger. Care must be taken by the spouse/partner not to overreact because it is an illness that she/he does not understand, especially after years of manic episodes have shown that the episodes are nothing to be scared of. Some episodes can be so "gentle" that they go undetected even in front of professionals in the field, as has been the case with many of mine. One could say the partner can "get used to it," though in all fairness, there may not be any getting used to it.

A double bind exists when the spouse/partner "accuses," or more accurately, presents the truth to the person that they are indeed in a manic state. This can be a damaging self-perception to the person, perceiving oneself to be in a serious, very undesirable emotional state. This can lead to feelings of rejection, which can be especially difficult in such a state of mind.

There comes a threshold, a "line" that, once it is crossed, you can no longer stop from entering the manic state.

How will I come down? Does it completely have a "will" of its own? Can I bring myself down, at least to a point? Or is it strictly a matter of it running its course? Is mania actually the more real state, in that it pulls you in, not because you are being a bad boy/girl and are putting yourself into it, but it in fact is your more natural state and therefore will sometimes pull you in toward it?

Exactly like my theory that my intelligence always pulls me through the manic door.

Or is it just the mania trying to prove itself? But what happens when the mania is successful in proving itself? According to the laws of logic and perception.

The real mystery is: how the manic state seems too real; how it has a life/will of its own; how it self-perpetuates and expands; how it ignores the evidence (internal "thoughts") to the contrary to persist as being so real and credible, and...

That I had had many of the DSM-IV symptoms exactly as described, completely shows/convinces me immediately after if not during coming down that I *obviously* was in a manic episode; this makes it *so much more* incredible that I was able to maintain the manic state for as long as I did.

Reasons Why I Need to Think of Myself as Being Intelligent, and Had to Develop Great Intelligence Self-Image as a Defense Mechanism Against the Feeling/Thought of Not Being So:

1. Parents: wanted me to be very intelligent, for good reasons, as well as to satisfy their egos of having a very intelligent son (cultural thing).
2. Competition against beast. To get the attention in the household, and defeat beast, *especially* when education was such a *huge* value in the family; to counteract my competitive complex.
3. My own self-motivation, caused by having done so well in school for years; the drive to thrive "intelligently" becomes "internalized," healthy in a way, and I became my own motivator to do well in school.

Therapy

Before beginning this section, I should state that the ideas below are based on my own experiences, gathered from years of being in therapy, and are not written by a licensed therapist. They are well thought-out, and I sincerely believe they are of value to the therapeutic community, both patients and therapists.

Therapy should most primarily be based on insight. Tracing the cause of a negative emotion/thought/behavior back to its roots, usually but not always in the person's family of origin, is necessary, in my opinion, to resolving the issue. It goes a tremendous way toward eradicating the effects of the original bad set of experiences.

The "tracing" back should be done as a cognitive act. I don't believe there is any need to "feel" the original causing situations, nor is there any need for the therapist to "drag and drudge up" the causing situation. The therapist can and should help the patient discover the cause-and-effect relationships on a cognitive level. Then the patient will have learned how and can do it by his/herself.

A single exercise of the "connection" will, of course, not make the issue, the current day negative emotion/thought/behavior, go away. Many "thought exercises" will, and the negative emotion will subside over time.

There is no one who cannot stand to gain from psychotherapy. In this day and age, the rapid pace of change over the past five decades has left the average person in a state of confusion and insecurity over the basic aspects of life, including relationships, job security, even basic survival. The human mind is a complex apparatus that, although capable of healing, can become unbalanced and easily distracted from the day-to-day functioning needed to cope with our complex world.

Modern psychotherapeutic techniques draw on solid principles gained from academic theory. The techniques also draw heavily on the clinical experience of many top therapists practicing in the field. Knowledge is exchanged through publications and conferences, as well as enormously through conversations between fellow practitioners. Many approaches have been tried over the years, and through the laws of trial and error, techniques have fallen by the wayside, but some have succeeded and developed.

A clinical psychologist is a highly educated individual. Years of graduate school are required in order to assume the role. Also, certainly not to be brushed aside, study is spent during the undergraduate years taking psychology and other related courses. Many, if not most, times, a thesis must be written that requires intensive in-depth work on a chosen topic. The psychotherapist must be accepted into the graduate program, which is a very competitive process with high requirements in terms of grades, course selection, and personal integrity. They take their education very seriously.

The obvious cannot be overstated. A therapist, clinical psychologist or otherwise, has chosen to dedicate their life to the most noble of causes, that of counseling those in emotional duress, aiding them to overcome what can and should be seen as life's most important challenges. They are exposed to the worst underside of life daily and must respond professionally as opposed to letting their own emotional reaction cloud the therapeutical process.

Psychotherapy has been around for a long time. For centuries, the human race has attempted to alleviate one another of one's psychological ailments. It has evolved rapidly over our lifetimes, along with the rapid cultural change that unfortunately makes psychotherapy necessary for many of us now. Many different ideas appeared especially in the late 60s and early 70s as our culture went through a period of expansion of consciousness and experimental ideas. As our culture stabilized afterward, in a relative sense, so did the approaches of clinicians and their techniques.

The approach of a psychotherapist can vary from individual-to-individual practitioner. Sometimes the same academic approach will vary. This does not imply that the therapist is not fully capable of treating the patient: quite to the contrary, the therapist develops their own style based upon their education and their experience as a practitioner. Some have a very intellectual approach, some are "warm and fuzzy," but various approaches can and do work well. There are many former patients who can testify to their positive experiences in therapy.

As with any developing field, there is always room for improvement. Some suggestions include:

1. There are certain areas of a person's life where the therapist should not intrude, unless the patient brings them up. One such example is the patient's sex life. This is a violation of the person's privacy.

2. The most serious problem I see with therapy is that the patient is hardly ever dismissed from therapy without an initiative first being taken on the part of the patient, such as he or she suggesting they are done, or simply getting up and walking out the door. When the patient has

reached the logical end of therapy, the therapist may reach for their two "aces in hole," asking, "How is your marriage?" then "How is your sex life?" when the possibility exists that even in the case of the therapist himself or herself, both might have something to be desired.

Psychotherapy is worth every dollar and every hour. At stake is your emotional well-being, which is very conceivably the most important part of your life. Many a rich person has entered therapy with their life in a state of shambles, willing to trade much of their wealth for peace of mind.

The therapist carries enormous responsibility, having your worst problems handed to them, your day-to-day well-being on their shoulders, having to handle emergencies of a critical nature. The utmost respect should be given to these people, the psychotherapists. It will enable the therapeutic process to function and make your lives a whole lot better.

Social-Learning Therapy

Therapy by Modeling; vicarious therapy; learning/advancing by observation.

Leading the Patient

The therapist should *tell* the patient what to do with his/her life situations when the situation is causing the patient enormous grief, such as when to end a very bad relationship. One time, I was going through two very bad relationships at once, one with a "girlfriend" and one with a "friend." The relationships were causing me an enormous number of problems and confusion. The therapist at the time was, of course, aware of this. But his approach was to "let me figure it out." So, for a couple years, I anguished in those two relationships. A couple years. Finally, I "figured out on my own" to get them out of my life, which immediately cleared up a lot of problems and was like a huge breath of fresh air in both cases.

I have also had therapists who immediately have recognized a detrimental situation and told me without hesitation to get out of damaging relationships. Not only did this immediately lift the enormous burden of a very poor relationship but also confirmed my belief that the individuals were possibly quite disturbed.

A strong gesture that a former patient can do is to actually correspond with their former therapist(s). Especially if it were a positive experience. An unfortunate part of being a therapist is that once a patient leaves therapy, the therapist almost always never hears about the extent that his or her efforts have been successful. I bet they would really like to see the outcome of their efforts over time, actualized in the former patient's real life. Possibly more significant, a bond has formed between the patient and therapist. This bond is, for all intents and purposes, a relationship. While the former patient may commonly avoid the former therapist because contact might create the self-perception of still being "sick," or in need of more therapy, the therapist is "left hanging" with an unknown bond, and most of all, not knowing how the person is currently doing. When I designed a computer system, I gained satisfaction in seeing it run successfully for years.

As a therapist expects a patient to divulge much, if not most, aspects of their personal life, and this is certainly essential to therapy, they should also ivulge some personal aspects of their own life. This will make the therapist appear very honest and open, which will help develop trust from the patient towards the therapist. This openness will also go a long way toward eradicating the air of superiority that inevitably shows up, the eradication of which will strongly progress and enhance the total therapeutic process.

I know this sounds like I'm monetizing therapy, but one way to think of your (possibly many) hours in therapy is to realize how much you spent on it over the years. That alone can help to bring you confidence that you have not only developed tools to cope and excel, but also to "be your own therapist."

You may sit for a whole hour and only come away with one valuable line. And that one line made the whole hour worthwhile.

In fact, you may take ten or twenty incredibly valuable lines from all of your therapeutic experience. And they will have enormous positive impacts on the rest of your life.

Take Notes During the Session

Recommendation: *take notes* during your session. I always have, and sections of the following self-help chapter are based on them. Taking notes in therapy is very effective in recalling the high points of a session and in being able to apply them to your life. You certainly would want to capture that one incredibly valuable line on paper. However, though notes can be clear, they do take moments away from the session, as well as stopping the flow of the conversation. But they are invaluable. I would always bring a notebook to my sessions, and often quickly write down key lines in my car after the concepts jelled.

Possibly record every session. At least in my case, the therapist's output at the end would often partially slip by me as in a rapid fashion. Had I recorded the sessions, I would have been able to play them back, pausing the player after significant statements for contemplation and absorption. I don't know how a therapist would feel about the session being recorded; it would be best to discuss it with him/her if you are interested in doing so and are going to devote the time and effort to listen to the playback.

Prepare for Sessions

Patient should *always* have topic(s), one or two, prepared for session. My therapists always complimented me on being "prepared." Most of the time a topic would come up during the week, and I would write it down. Sometimes I would think of one on the way to the session.

Coming into a session and just sitting there places a burden on the therapist, and though a good therapist can always productively open the session, the patient having a significant topic makes for a very energetic and useful start.

Issues with Cognitive Therapy

Cognitive Therapy, or CT, is very much in use today by clinical psychologists and associated therapists. It is an "active" therapy in that it depends on the patient performing an action. Its premise is that a negative emotion is tied to a negative thought. The action that the patient performs is to "replace" the negative thought with a positive one, or at least "negate" the negative thought, thereby getting rid of the negative emotion, and possibly creating a positive emotion.

Its popularity is due to the fact that it works. It works in many people across many situations. Many therapists are trained in how to administer it, as it is the "therapy of the day," until something comes along that is better.

I have been fortunate enough to have been treated by a psychologist who had not only been trained in CT but used it extensively in his practice.

Contrary to CT theory, however, I find that no matter how many times I negate a particular negative thought, the negative thought never completely goes away, meaning that it continues to reoccur. The model I was presented with in therapy was analogous to a neural network in AI (artificial intelligence).

In this model, the brain/mind has a collection of pathways that, when acting together, have "learned" a particular response to what it is presented with. It has been "trained," or taught, the response based on the perception. What it is presented with in psychology can be called a "stimulus," and the "response" in this case would be the negative thought/emotion. As an example, the stimulus might be something like someone looking away from you when you say something, and the response would be your thought, "I am boring, uninteresting, unintelligent." You have "learned" this untrue response through various ways, possibly with its roots in childhood ridicule, possibly by comparing yourself to how you unrealistically imagine some other people to be. People on TV are not that way all the time in real life.

In AI, the stimulus is called the "input," and the response is called the "output." For example, in a self-driving car, a red traffic light would be the input, and the output would be stopping the car. The neural network would be "trained," or taught, by showing it many, many different pictures of red lights, and then telling it to stop the car after each picture. The power, or intelligence, of the network is that after being presented, or trained, by the many pictures of red lights, and telling it to stop after each one, the network will then be able to infer, or extrapolate what it has learned onto pictures of red lights that it has not been presented with.

In the psychological model, a person might have been ridiculed to the point where they have learned or developed a complex. Then, later in life, when presented with a situation that *looks* similarly negative and *can* be interpreted that way, the person will interpret it that way because that is how they learned it, when in fact, there is no basis for it in reality.

In the neural network analogy in cognitive therapy that I was presented with, the psychological network becomes "retrained." That is, you eventually "unlearn" the negative response.

However, in me, I have observed that the network never becomes fully retrained to the point of unlearning the response. (Note that this might vary due to the strength and severity of the negatively learned response.)

What does happen however, is that, over time, *it takes a lot quicker* for me to negate the negative thought. Or even substitute a positive one. Also, the negation becomes very "solidified" once it has been done.

As an example, seeing someone turning their head when I speak, and being met with a negative thought/emotion, would instantly be replaced with "someone just entered the room and the person I was speaking to turned their head to see who was present at the social gathering, which is a perfectly natural thing to do," and the negative emotion would cease.

The second issue I see with cognitive therapy centers on the therapist. The therapist, no doubt, uses it on him/herself. If you, for example, are a mason that has been trained to build beautiful patios for customers, there are strong odds that you have done masonry for your property as well.

With a therapist and CT, however, when the therapist performs CT on themselves, they are dealing with a mind most often not burdened with maladies that have brought someone into therapy. Also, the therapist has been specifically professionally trained in CT. The patient, however, has "illnesses" in the mind that warrant coming into therapy in the first place; and these cognitive shortcomings, though usually temporary in nature, can inhibit, possibly greatly inhibit, the learning of the methods needed to perform cognitive therapy.

When you "negate a thought," but then follow up the negation with a thought/feeling such as, "No, maybe it *is* real," referring to the original negative thought, then in fact, what happened is that you encountered a particularly strong negative thought. When you become psychologically strong enough, and you encounter that situation, you "plug-in" or follow up the "No, maybe it IS real," with the thought, "It was a strong one." For me, this has always gotten me out of the original negative, stronger-than-most, thought/feeling, once I have mastered it.

Two-Minute Drill

Recommendation: at one point, when you have been in therapy for quite a while, ask the therapist to do a "15-minute" summary of your overall psychological state, i.e., your condition.

This can provide for you a very useful "guide" that will be valuable for the rest of your life. It can summarize your condition as observed by the therapist over a significant period of time. It will raise your self-awareness, which is a gateway to building a better self.

It is especially important to write down the "two-minute drill" as it should be something you would want to refer to over the years. I filled an entire page, and the page was so valuable I made a photocopy, uploaded it to the cloud, kept it accessible, and referred to it often to the point that I memorized it.

Assertiveness Training

Best form of therapy/behavior for interpersonal interaction.

Start off kind, then *gradually* build up "strength," assertiveness. Do not become "aggressive" until all other approaches have failed.

Conceive Therapy as "School"

You are there partially to learn how to use the process of therapy in the future, as well as to benefit from it while in it.

A perfect example is CT. It takes a long time (years) for it to become effective/functional in most every situation. In therapy, you learn the technique in theory and by successfully applying it in a relatively small number of situations.

When a new patient begins the significant part of the first session with a statement similar to, "and here is what is really bothering me," or if the therapist is wise enough to begin the significant part of the first session with a statement similar to "what bothers you the most," not only should the therapist pay incredibly careful attention to what he or she says, but you should *follow up* on that very topic at least every other session until the matter is cleared up. When the patient conveys their #1 problem that they are willing to talk about, they are being very serious, and the matter conveyed should have high priority over others.

When a patient brings up a serious issue that they are dealing with, and the issue has been dealt with in therapy many, many times, but the patient brings it up once again, the patient should not be greeted with the line, "Come on now, we've beat that one to death," or "Let's move on." Rather:

    1. It is obvious that the matter is extremely important to the patient, and

    2. The matter is yet to be resolved.

For those two reasons, it becomes obvious that the issue deserves further attention, conceivably more so than any other.

The therapist must draw on their huge reservoir of patience to deal with a seemingly repetitive situation that presents the illusion that no progress has been made. However, from my personal experience, amazing breakthroughs can and are made after conceivably years of hashing over and over the same issue.

The therapist must have a reservoir of knowledge on many subjects because he/she could be confronted with anything from the world of life. If they are to dive into the entire life of the patient to make "repairs," they need to have a broad and deep base on as everything as possible. For example, if the patient says, "I am indecisive about buying a house, but I think I really want one," he/she should not jump at the first house the patient finds but evaluate with the patient if that house is really a good match for the patient.

The Over-Attribution of Patient's Psychological Phenomena to "Mother"
Psychoanalytical theory is handed down from Freud. In my earlier years, my brother was much more a negative influence on me than my mother, who was also somewhat, but certainly not completely, negative. But in therapy, my therapist, who, in looking back was quite skilled, attributed more of my issues to my mother than to my brother.

A Significant Problem with Therapy
A big problem with therapy is how, in the session, they focus on "the problem of the day" rather than on ongoing, very serious issues. Stating that they are getting to "a core issue" through "the problem of the day" can have quite a bit of truth to it, yet dealing directly with an issue is perhaps more effective. Perhaps a hybrid approach works, where the day's problem is traced to the person's core issues. However, the central issues should and need to be addressed on a constant and complete basis. Especially, daily "band-aids" are worthless and a waste of everyone's time. Many times, when the band-aid approach was taken with me, the issue might come back within the time it took for me to drive back to work.

On Sep 25, 2017, at 10:46 AM, Michael Lazaar <michael.lazaar@gmail.com> wrote:

Facilitated by 1) knowledge of how childhood/upbringing/family of origin affected you 2) you must be able to "trace" your current day issues back to their original "childhood etc." causes "traumatic" negative causes of current day problems can be caused by any phenomenon up to the present day, i.e., not just childhood. For ex., a very bad relationship in early adulthood can have a very negative effect later in life.

Single Visit Therapist Visits

The concept of therapy-on-demand, just like making an appointment at a family practice. You would make the appointment with the therapist on an as-needed basis. Like going to a doctor once or twice a year, for something acute.

Like having to make a big decision, which can be made, or greatly assisted, in one (two-hour) session.

The weekly visits would end much sooner.

Issues such as: availability in therapist's schedule versus urgency of need of visit. The trick is to keep the therapist's schedule with enough open spots in a given day to accommodate the patients.

Should there be a "middle ground"-type setup for in-between issues that are too big for one visit, that can wait approximately two days, which don't need the "Therapist Emergency Room," but don't require months or years of therapy?

An ancillary issue of therapy is the "lack of specialization," the "one size fits all" phenomenon such as the therapist does not specialize only in bipolar disorder.

In a perfect world, it would be beneficial, I think, if a therapist were to follow the patient around *in their environment, such as the (corporate) workplace*, so the therapist can experience the patient's actual environment instead of within the confines of the therapist's office. Maybe to experience the patient's environment, be it the patient's workplace wherever it may be, or in fact any environment of the patient, for example: driving the kids, shopping, etc. I would recommend the therapist doing this on occasion during the year.

Developing Tools in Therapy

After many years of therapy, you should definitely have developed the *tools* to help you get through every situation you will encounter. You can stay in therapy the rest of your life, but in my opinion, as someone who's been through it, you will be wasting your time, your money, and the therapist's time.

Marijuana in Therapy

One of the *most amazing* things about the experience of my manic state is how many of my *problems seem to go away in the sense that they are now seen to be not real, "inverted," as in "super-cognitive therapy." If you could somehow safely*

induce this state in therapy, such as with marijuana, then you would have an amaz-
ing therapeutic tool! Marijuana has this property.

My very first visit to a therapist was sophomore year. I told him, "I had been se-lectively removed from the gene pool" (for being abnormal, and for abnormal be-havior). It was a very Stanford student statement. He laughed in my face. Not a good way to be introduced to the world of clinical therapy.

At the risk of sounding cliché, in order for therapy to be successful, you have to want it to be. As excellent as your therapist probably is, not only do you have to be dedicated to improving yourself through the therapeutic process, but, at least in my case, I did more of the work myself. With expert guidance from an excellent, very intelligent person who dedicated his life to study and improving the lives of others.

Self-Help
Before beginning this section, I wish to emphatically state that these self-help "tools" work and have been of enormous value to me. As I have noted above pre-ceding my ideas on therapy, the tools and concepts below are not being presented by a licensed therapist. However, they were formed over the years, both while in therapy and not. They have been carefully developed and tested across many sit-uations. They should be of value to anyone, including but certainly not limited to someone currently enjoying the therapeutic process.

Core Feelings
A foundation of cognitive therapy is that of the "core belief." As I agree with the basic concept, I think that such an entity is more of an emotional phenomenon than a cognitive one. It is for this reason that, at least to myself, I have renamed "core beliefs" to "core feelings."

Examples of core feelings are:
- "I am inferior."
- "I am worthless."
- "There is something wrong with/about me."
- "I have a bad life" (an especially common one, I believe).

- "I have a boring life."
- "I am small/little." (In fact, when you were very young, you were littler than everyone around you).
- "I am incompetent."
- "I am lonely, insignificant, unimportant."
- "I am skill-less, talentless."
- "I am a bad parent."
- "Nobody likes me."
- "It's my fault."
- "I made so many wrong decisions."

The two main characteristics to realize about these core feelings is that

1. More people have them then you think, and
2. They are false.

They emanate from childhood where a person was "put down" by peers, parents, and most of all, siblings. They have become internalized, meaning that when the criticism had been thrown at you, you came to believe them because at the time, you were not wise enough to recognize the source as being incorrect, as being jealous, as being harmful, sometimes intentionally so.

In my experienced opinion, as I have dealt with some of these core feelings, they can be conquered by most of all recognizing them. Then, through the insight gained by realizing their origin, and subsequent falsehood, you no longer have to live with them as the determining factor of your emotional wellbeing.

The core feeling of, "I have a bad life," is especially dangerous because it can lead to jealousy. A person can get jealous of anyone he/she perceives to have a good life. And probably many others have the same complex as you. No lives are super-great, and few are super-bad.

I used to occasionally have a syndrome which I call "summer depression." Its core feeling is "I have a bad life," in the summer because:

1. There are a limited number of "beautiful summer Sundays," and
2. Most everyone is either at a barbecue, a country club drinking vodka gimlets, a weekend trip, gone somewhere nice, down at the shore, or some other great social activity.

I do wonder what the truth is: if most people are doing these great things, or if it is just my imagination emanating from that core feeling. And suddenly I hear a lawn mower on a Sunday afternoon. And realizing that the roads are empty, not because everyone drove to somewhere great, but they are sitting home watching baseball or golf (which is an absolutely fine thing to do in my opinion). Or vacuuming or at the mall. And it makes me feel much better.

As a very important epilogue to the concept of a core feeling, in the "center" of all core feelings, I place the central core feeling of "I am bad." Outward from this central core feeling come all other negative core feelings, like spokes on a wheel. The core feeling of "I am bad" is a "synthesis" of all core feelings and is also caused by the same causes of core feelings: being put down by siblings, peers, and parents.

Throwing a Template (and Feeling and Perception Must Match)
It is obvious that a perception can produce a feeling, an emotion. A perception of a beautiful garden produces a feeling of wonderment and tranquility. A perception of a professional football field produces a feeling of excitement. A perception of an auto accident produces a feeling of horror and caution. And a perception of looking at a clock after you woke up, depending on the time, may make you feel tired by making you think you didn't get enough sleep even if you were well-rested.

I believe there to be a fundamental "rule" that perceptions and feelings must match, (most of the time). I therefore believe that perception-feeling causality works in the opposite direction as well. A feeling can produce a perception. A perfect example is that of a very strong feeling, in some individuals, producing a hallucination. I believe that this is what explains and produces a hallucination: a strong feeling projecting outward. It may *appear* that the hallucination precedes/causes the emotion, but in fact, it's the other way around: the feeling/emotion is so strong that it causes the hallucination, so that the perception and feeling match.

Now, take the specialized case of what I call "Throwing a Template." I use this phrase in the context of when a person has a strong feeling inside of them, such as a core feeling, they will "throw a template," or impose a perception, to match the core feeling. The core feeling, "I am incompetent," will throw a template on a situation that will then reinforce the person's belief, no matter how incorrect. This core feeling emanates from the person's past, yet the constant reinforcement perpetuates it to the current day.

Based on a strong emotion, you create a perception that does not exist. Here is an example from my work life:

1. My director sends me an email with a positive complement.
2. I feel a rush of approval.
3. However, since I have a core feeling of rejection from a teacher in the past, this core feeling puts me into a director-me state of disapproval.
4. From that state, I take the feeling of disapproval and impose a perception back onto the email, which suddenly becomes a lot less "good," a lot less approving.

So, it can be seen that the core feeling throws a template which creates a self-perception of disapproval, causing a negative feedback-loop, when in fact the original source of the perception was approval.

Here is another example of "throwing a template," here seen to involve pathologizing the manic state, and how it can be harmful to yourself and your sense of accomplishment:

1. You receive a huge compliment from a well-respected neighbor. In this example, the compliment is genuinely huge, for example on your entire career.
2. You *naturally* get very excited.
3. Much later, perhaps a day or so, you find yourself in a calm state.
4. You look back at the compliment as not meaning that much. Because you feel calmer, you now perceive the compliment as being less significant. In other words, you "throw the template," or create the perception, of a less significant compliment to match the feeling or state that you are in.
5. You then *attribute* the *initial perception* of the compliment and *subsequent high-energy reaction* to a manic-assisted state, and therefore an underserved reaction that inflated the original perception of the compliment. Because you now think, from a lower energy state, that a manic-induced high energy reaction caused a false perception.
6. You have *pathologized* the reaction and therefore reduced the compliment when in fact, it was genuinely very strong.

Email itself lends itself to the concept of "throwing a template." It is said that a problem with an email is that it does not contain a lot of expression that normally accompanies interpersonal communication. It therefore can lend itself to misinterpretation. This can function like a Rorschach test in psychology. (A Rorschach test is where a subject is shown inkblots; then their perceptions of the inkblots are analyzed using psychological interpretation. It is used to examine a person's personality characteristics and emotional functioning.) A person can "read into" an email emotions, in some cases upsetting negative ones like anger, that aren't there.

In fact, the phenomenon of "throwing a template" can explain how a Rorschach test functions.

A Thought is a Perception

As an extension of the "rule" that feeling and perception must match, look at a thought as being a perception. There is no doubt as to the interplay between thoughts and emotion: a thought can certainly cause an emotion, and an emotion can cause a thought. This is, in fact, the basis of cognitive therapy: that, in ordinary circumstances, a negative emotion causes a negative thought. It is by substituting a positive thought, which is seen here to be a positive perception, that the thought-perception changes the negative emotion into a positive one.

Feeling and Self-Perception

As a special case, a feeling and self-perception must match as well. In classic self-perception, if a person with no prior political preference either way for a particular candidate is told to read out loud a statement supporting the candidate, the person, after reading the statement will claim to support the candidate.

Conversely, a person who has been falsely arrested and possibly incarcerated will perceive himself to be a criminal and then internalize it. Due to his/her feeling, the self-image of being a criminal will then be projected outward in that the person is more likely to adopt criminal behavior and perform criminal acts in order to create the self-perception of being a criminal, to agree with their internal state.

"THAT"

I've noticed another very interesting phenomenon involving perception and emotion. It states that strong perceptions can cause emotions that only need to last momentarily. But instead, they can linger for a very long time. For example, you might be looking over your VISA statement and notice an unusually high charge (nothing screamingly high, but higher than average). You might react with the thought-feeling, "Oh no, I'm going broke." And you might then make the mistake of carrying this thought-feeling with you for quite a while, conceivably hours. But the truth is, you have greatly exaggerated your reaction, your reaction to this single perception.

The point is that the emotional reaction was not caused by any condition or circumstances over a significant period of time. It was caused by a momentary perception. It can be misconstrued as being a permanent condition which will then lead to the thought/emotion of it being a permanent state. When in fact, it was only one moment.

If you could train yourself to say to yourself "THAT" (or whatever works for you) every time you catch a negative emotional reaction, in most all of the cases you will find the perception that caused the negative emotion. This immediately makes the negative emotion go away because you don't attribute it to anything of permanence. (Once again, this assumes that the perception was not of a serious event, but still strong enough to cause an emotional reaction.)

Once the true cause is identified, the emotion goes away because your mind sees no reason for it to linger. It is a variation of "perception causes feeling." Everything sort of gets "cleaned up." Once the "THAT" is identified, it can be dealt with in a mature manner, if not eradicated. (Constantly) Identifying the "source" of "THAT" may seem like a burden at first, but it is enormously helpful and will almost immediately impact your emotional life.

"STATE" —- (Run-On)

Related to the concept that how a perception causes an emotion that need only last a moment, but can linger, is what I call "State." By example, there was a person I used to work with who had a poor reputation because he was difficult to work with and narcissistic, among other reasons. When forced to think of this person, I would have negative thoughts and emotions. This phenomenon, I realized, was best seen as putting me into a specific, in this case negative, frame, or "state," of mind. The key attributes are that not only was it a negative state of mind, but that it was momentary. By recognizing it as having entered a particular, specific State, I would say the word "State" to myself and leave the negative thought/feeling behind me as I moved onto the next thought.

Related to the concept of State, is what I call "Run-on." I noticed this when my attention would be drawn to the negative person mentioned in the paragraph above, and subsequently I would enter the negative state. Then, when I thought immediately afterwards of a different colleague, I would also think of this person in a negative light, when in fact, the colleague was great to work with, very bright, and a good friend. In other words, the State would perpetuate itself even when the negative perception was removed, and the new perception was undeserving of the negative thought/emotion. When I caught myself doing this, I would say to myself "Run-On," and the second, underserved negative attitude would disappear.

Another example of run-on is when someone extends a person's state much further back through time than is accurate. For example, a person may be behaving hypomanic on a given day. An observer sees the person in this state and claims that the hypomanic person has actually been in that state for much longer.

Time Perspective

In my long but very rewarding journey of self-improvement, I have come across another tool that I have used. I call it "time perspective." It is this simple: the length of time that you adopt to view your life, the perceptions in your life, and the events in your life, affects the emotions that result from what it is you are viewing.

In this model, I create, or discover, two timeframes. One I call the "long-looking frame," and the other I call the "short-looking frame."

When my view would use the "short frame," I noticed the following:

1. I would attribute meaning to situations that had none.
2. I was mistrusting.
3. I would attribute negative motivations to others.
4. I entered a "pass-fail" mode, as in, "I made a super contribution" to a project, or none at all.
5. I could become uptight.
6. My mind could start to thrash, or speed.
7. Every single perception would count so much and lead to a strong response.
8. I would throw templates-perceptions "wildly."
9. Most of all, my perceptions would be over a short span of time, which ignores the stability of a long-time perspective.

But the attributes of the "long-looking frame" were quite different. The "long-looking frame" was characterized most of all as being a relaxed state. In that state, I noticed the following:

1. People were of no threat to me.
2. I saw the positive side of people.
3. I saw that people were capable of, and most always had, positive motivations for their actions.
4. I would make varying degrees of contribution to a work project, without being a star, or the person who held the project back.
5. I saw that, in work projects, there really are no stars or failures, and that everyone makes a worthwhile contribution.
6. I had a stable mind!
7. I would have what I call a "gyroscopic" effect, in that I would be well-centered, and whenever I would be pulled off my center, I would, at times quickly, come back to it.

The Executioner

Through my growing up, there were two or three people who criticized me quite a bit. Of course, the criticism was not deserved anywhere near the extent that once was given, if at all. Mostly, not at all.

However, the constancy of it became internalized. Due to it, I at times was quick to view my work as being inadequate when in fact, it wasn't at all. This phenomenon can go as deep as creating a negative self-image close to the core of your being.

An effect of this is that a "slice" of positively motivated behavior almost immediately is covered up by a negative attribution – by the executioner.

Once you have successfully eradicated yourself, to hopefully a great extent, of attributing negative causes to your motivations and actions, don't make the common mistake of attributing negative causes to the motivations and actions of others. Even once you clean up your self-perception of why you do and think things, there is a tendency to continue to suspect others of thinking they have negative motivations, either consciously or unconsciously, for their actions. Once you do see your true, positive side and how it dominates, your next logical, very beneficial step is to see it in others and correctly attribute it to others.

A very hard attribution "riddle": To discern when the cause of a negative emotion is due to the current perception only, the "that," or when it is also due to your past. You always should look at the present perception; it at least "triggered" the emotion emanating from the past or is the sole cause of the current emotion.

High/Low

This is the phenomenon of comparing two things that are or can be related in some way. The mistake is made in comparing the least desirable traits or state of the one you are currently pre-occupied with, with the most desirable traits or attributes of the other.

By example, when studying your job or position, there is a state where you see it as very undesirable. In that state, you are preoccupied with the most negative attributes of the job.

Then you compare it to a different job or position. But mistakenly, you compare your current job's negative traits to the most positive ones of the other job. In this light, your current job will most likely be seen as being dismal when compared to this other job or position.

In this case, you are making the mistake of "high/low," or comparing the lowest elements of one thing to the highest of another. You will always come up very short. When the reality is, both items in the comparison have both high- and low-ends, and a full spectrum in-between.

This cognitive phenomenon can be applied to many, many other cases, such as, unfortunately, spouses. There's always that "one who got away." Since we know our spouse very well, there does exist the reality that we know his/her faults quite well. There is a possible tendency to compare the "low-end" of our spouse to the positive real and/or imaginary traits of the "fantasy spouse"; this is a strong example of high/low.

Reset Button

Once a certain degree of "stabilization" is reached, involving a "cognitive system/structure" categorized by conclusions that have been reached through a long span, possibly years, of thought and therapy, the person should be able to, in times of uncertainty and doubt, push a "cognitive reset button" which takes him/her back to the state of advancement and stability that has been reached over time.

Yeah But…

Along the lines of cognitive therapy, I have come to use a very useful tool. I call it "yeah but."

It fits into the cognitive therapy framework in many ways. Firstly, I noticed it came up in my thoughts when I would have a knee-jerk reaction to a thought about an accomplishment. For example, I would have a thought about having completed a project back in AT&T involving placing a color laser printer on the department TCP/IP LAN (an internet transportation language on a local network, much like your home Wi-Fi, if you have it). That thought was then followed by one of the projects being quite successfully done. Then after that thought, I have the thought "yeah but…" a thought when completed, degrades the accomplishment for any given reason.

As examples: when looking back at my J&J career, I will think of the very high admiration my two key "customers" had for me. Customers in the sense that they were the primary recipients of my delivered work, as they were the heads of the storage team in N.A. (North America) and EMEA (Europe, the Middle East, and Africa) respectively. But then immediately after this positive thought comes into my head, I think, "Yeah but… they weren't high-level management."

As another example, I will think that although my best times were run in championship meets, when I think of a very good performance in a dual meet (which is between two teams instead of many teams as in a championship meet), I think, "Yeah but… it was just a dual meet." Perhaps a professional athlete might have the same thought: when thinking of a great game, he/she might think "Yeah, but…it was the regular season, it wasn't the playoffs."

I have come to realize that the popping into my head of the "yeah but…" was "simply" my way of putting down the accomplishment, the putting down of which had roots in negative moments of my life involving criticism which I internalized, and in fact has no basis for truth in current reality.

In keeping with the concept of cognitive therapy, I then learned to negate the negative thought involving degradation of an accomplishment by 1) ignoring it, and 2) realizing that the accomplishment was, in fact, positive and worthy of the praise I received for it.

Then, as the last and most powerful piece of the cognitive therapy process, I learned to focus on the specific phrase "yeah but…" Now, whenever this phrase pops into my head, I immediately negate it and realize the accomplishment for what it was.

Being able to train yourself to catch the "yeah but," or whatever your possibly many erroneous automatic responses are, and stop them from influencing your original positive meaning, works. I recommend starting with one negative phrase only.

As an important epilogue to "yeah but," I have had rare instances where a "yeah but" did not work, i.e., it was followed by a second "yeah but." I have learned that this is "simply" due to the force of the criticism being especially strong. However, the accomplishment still stands as is, so all I do is negate the second "yeah but," and everything is fine. Sort of like bringing in the ninth-inning closer. Also, I have never had to do a third "yeah but." The second one has always worked if the first one didn't.

Look at the Data

Instead of agonizing over something, anything, examine the unbiased, unaltered truth and reality of the situation. Often, this refers to something that was said.

Don't put thoughts in a person's head. You don't know what the other person is thinking. Don't assume that the person is thinking a negative thought about you; don't assume anything about what the other person is thinking.

Do not throw a template that originates from erroneous feelings onto a situation, and then misinterpret the situation. Emotions are not necessarily accurate representations of reality. A negative emotion will distort a situation by a template being thrown that then creates an inaccurate perception of the situation. In many cases, a situation that appears to cause grief in fact, if properly interpreted, will not if the simple truth of the situation is seen.

Erroneous Negative Spin-Out of Thought

Pay special attention to those "moments" in your thought-stream when your thoughts instantly speed up into a negative spiral. They are an entrance into erroneous thinking.

The key here are two components:

1. An erroneous, negative thought about yourself, and
2. The thought rapidly spins, almost out of control.

In these circumstances, the original thought should be completely disregarded as being a false thought. It will then disappear, and you should continue on your path of the thought-train you had been on.

Rejection vs Permanence

Here's something to keep in mind when dealing with feelings of rejection, which many of us experience from time to time. This is not referring to the rejection that might occur when attempting to initiate a romantic relationship, but rather the emotion of rejection occasionally felt in a day-to-day relationship. A specific example would be a new but stable relationship that has entered a steadier state.

Once a relationship has reached that steady state, it becomes extremely likely that the other person is not suddenly going to wake up one morning and not like you. Once the relationship has been established, the other person has solidified their feelings and thoughts toward you and is not going to suddenly decide that you are unworthy of their affection and trust.

There can be temporary variances in the attitudes toward you, if you did or said something absolutely deserving of a momentary flare-up, but even then, the animosity will not be a deep-seated one, and be temporary in nature (unless there have been *many repeated* negative incidents).

Holding onto this knowledge, the awareness of the permanence of a relationship, is also very useful in a long-term relationship, which will add greatly to the stability of the relationship and remove any emotional roller-coaster that no one likes to be on.

Pathologizing

We pathologize so many things. (I'm almost sure it's we and not just I.)

Examples of Pathologizing

Fantasy/dreaming is a motivator. Why is fantasy a "dirty" word? (Why does it have negative connotations?) Because it was (is) a Freudian defense mechanism, and Freud put his defense mechanisms in a somewhat pathological context, at best as a healthy adaptation to a personal or social ill.

When someone cares about you, it's a very special thing.

A good friend of mine once sent me religious material. I asked him if he sent them to everyone he knew, or just me. He replied that he was sending them to just me.

This gave me the feeling that he really cared about me. I then felt that when someone cares about you, it's a very special thing. That person becomes very special to you. It then flashed through my mind that the reason why I felt so special when I had this feeling that someone cared about me is because I had such a low self-image, and that this positive affirmation was negating that. That I "had climbed out of my hole" and therefore bringing myself up to a good level of self-respect, which was causing me more pleasure than was due. In fact, a therapist of mine had remarked, correctly, that I am very sensitive to both praise and criticism.

However, the idea of taking the concept of having someone caring for a person, a beautiful human trait, and the naturally wonderful response it brings, and pathologizing the response to be the by-product of emotional damage was a very sad thing. Fortunately, I have trained myself to recognize pathologizing. That ability leads to a much healthier outlook.

A Matter of Degree

It is agreeably a matter of degree by which the line is set on the scale between "normalcy" and "pathology," whereas the place on the scale determines the presence of the illness, if any. (Note the *binary* implication of the use of the word "presence" to dramatize the concept of *being normal* or *not.*) The truth, in my opinion, is that the medical establishment, and also therapeutic establishment, places that line too far toward the pathology side.

A perfect example of pathologizing: I was about to eat ice cream one evening, so I went to the silverware drawer to get a spoon. We have several types of spoons in our drawer. I selected one of the types of a "large spoon with a heavy weight" to eat the ice cream with. As I sat down, I observed once again how selective I am in choosing what piece of silverware I use at any given time.

This time, however, I had the thought of how peculiar it is that I always put the effort in to choose what I perceive to be the optimal match of that type of silverware for that moment. I then immediately thought of the behavior as being "neurotic," hence "pathological," and looked toward the psychiatric establishment for the explanation of this behavior.

Then, as I have trained myself to do using cognitive therapy, I immediately challenged the thought that the behavior was pathological, as I have trained myself against believing that some of what I think and do is pathological.

I then immediately thought of some of the finer restaurants I eat at, and how they set the place settings with different size silverware, such as a smaller fork for salad and a larger fork for the main course! In fact, I then realized that the finer the restaurant, the more attention is paid to the specific type of silverware used for every single serving.

So then, I was able to realize that I was merely emulating fine dining, which is a far step from pathologizing a behavior.

Last night, I read that a *symptom* of mania is "hypergraphics," or compulsive writing. So, due to the laws of self-perception, I perceived myself as having compulsive writing. The next morning, for the first time in about a month, I write (in more than one "document"). This could be due to:

- I perceive myself now as a compulsive writer, so now I (must) write.
- I now feel myself to be a writer, so I have to write (throw the template; *create a self-perception)* to agree with my internal state/feeling.

A symptom (not mine) of hypergraphics is "writing in spirals." My desire to use *italics,* **bold,** [brackets], etc. in my more creative writing can be seen as compulsiveness in writing a certain way.

However, the Wikipedia page said that the "pathology" is caused by a condition in the prefrontal lobes. And that bipolar disorder can "cause" the "large amount of writing."

But an attribute of bipolar disorder is known to be *creativity*. Therefore, if writing can be seen as a creative act/behavior, as I believe in general it is, my writing is now seen as being a product of my (hypomanic) <u>enhanced creativity</u>, *not* "forced writing." In fact, not even hypomanic!

In this new light, the use of **bold**, <u>underline</u>, *italics,* [ ], etc., etc., can now be seen, as I have said all along, as a writing *art form*, an individual, unique, and original *creative expression*. I just wonder how many other people's "compulsive writing," such as writing in spirals, writing backwards, etc., should be seen more as a creative expression and much less as *pathologizing*.

Try this: whenever you observe anything that you attach a pathological attribution to, try doing a cognitive thought substitution, substituting the healthy reason for the initially perceived unhealthy one.

Psychology

Why do people think that a thought-feeling that emanated from the unconscious mind is necessarily negative? For that matter, why do people think that power has to be intrinsically negative as well? The unconscious might very well be filled with positive intentions, motivations, drives, and emotions. For example, unconsciously, people strive to educate themselves, and in fact, self-education is rewarded internally by positive emotions. Therefore, if self-education is viewed as a valued drive, then the fact that it is positively rewarded by the person shows that the unconscious drive to self-educate is a positive drive.

Similarly, power is most often thought of as a negative attribute. It is often associated with rulers with bad intent, selfish corporate executives out for their own gain regardless of what they inflict on the people who report up to them, etc.

However, most everyone if not everyone who was at one time or currently is in a "power hierarchy" knew their direct supervisor quite well. While some people have had negative experiences due to poor performance, even those with poor performance reports might have had their supervisor deliver the "bad" news in a humane, constructive way. Many, if not most, people have had good, if not very good, relationships with their supervisor, if not with many of them. This reality holds up all the way up the line. When you look at the actual reality of your relationship with your supervisor, you will probably realize it wasn't bad after all, if not quite possibly very positive. This holds true all the way up the line.

In governments, try to imagine that the Head of State actually has the best interests of their constituency as their primary motive. He/she seems to spend an incredible, if not an enormous, amount of effort and time, improving the well-being of their country. Though it may seem that Heads of State are only out to hold onto and increase their power, when examined closely, their actions and decisions are seen to benefit the people of their country. This is especially true economically, as the health of an economy is directly tied to the standard of living of the populace, which is of utmost importance. As an example: a populist. A populist attempts to please as many of the people as possible: to become "as popular" as possible with therefore as many people as possible. This results in pleasing, fulfilling the wishes and direction of a very large percentage of the population.

It is (quite) possible that someone who has *learned power* will "lock, pursue" that end/goal, as opposed to someone who hasn't learned power. Power can be and usually is a behavior that is rewarding to the individual, and therefore is propagated. The main point here is that the person who learned power will become "stuck" in the behavior-motivation-pursuit of power, as opposed to the person who hasn't learned power, and/or has risen above it, and will be motivated by more cooperative (as opposed to competitive), *positive* behavior/attitudes.

For example, older siblings tend to learn power, then be locked into its pursuit. The same goes for people who were physically larger than their peers as children. This is a major criticism of our and other countries' political system, in that our leaders want power and therefore to at least to some extent have not risen above its behavior cycle to more beneficial, "humanitarian goals."

The world theater is now seen as one where the leadership of the world is driven by people motivated by the acquisition of power, as opposed to people *only* truly concerned for the welfare of all. However, being a power seeker and obtaining power is not necessarily a bad trait. It also can be very beneficial to the country. Power can be, and in many cases is, a positive trait, with good intentions. But it in and of itself is seen as not the most optimal state. A famous line: "Never elect someone to office who wants it."

Can the drive for power be something more than just compensation for feelings of powerlessness/inferiority?

Which is a stronger drive, the drive to retain and protect the power you have or the drive to acquire more of it?

By acquiring more power, you retain the power you have. By simply retaining power, you don't acquire any more. As I wrote above, I see power also as a learned behavior which therefore is modified over time, which therefore can continue to become more civilized.

A basic problem with most of the excellent research done by academic psychologists is that it doesn't seem to go anywhere. Meaning, the results of the research don't appear to enter mainstream society, in fact, not even the fringes. Except for an occasional article on the internet, the public is usually not even aware nor certainly affected by their research. In my opinion, and I feel this is justified, not only as someone who studied academic psychology but as a thinking person who sees the benefit to society, the psychological research that has been accepted as being accurate and worthy by the field should be used to enact laws by Congress.

Another use of academic research, and there are many, is that no one should be permitted to become a manager of people at a company until they have been taught Zimbardo's famous Prison Experiment. In the experiment, a simulated prison was built in Jordan Hall, which is the location of the Psychology Department at Stanford University. The experiment randomly separated a group of people into two groups. One group was assigned to be the prison guards; the other group was assigned to be the prisoners. The people in the experiment were not actual prisoners in real life, i.e., they had not committed any crime; they just were randomly assigned to the role of prisoners. Same with the prison guards: they were not trained to be guards; they were simply randomly assigned that role.

Within days, the guards were treating the prisoners very harshly. Certainly, for no behavior on the part of the prisoners that in any way justified such treatment.

How does this relate to management, in business or any other field where managers are found? Assigning someone a management position can be seen as assigning them the authority of a prison guard. I have often seen the management position abused, as I'm sure most of you have who have in some time in your career reported to someone. Such exposure and training in Zimbardo's Prison Experiment would go a long way in eradicating such abuse. That is but one example of a practical application of the thousands of psychology experiments and research papers performed and written over the years.

"Active" Self-Perception

The following describes what I call "active self-perception": instead of simply perceiving yourself performing a behavior, then forming a belief/conclusion about yourself based on that self-perception, you intentionally, or *actively*, perform a behavior, specifically to create a self-perception which creates a thought/emotion (or may agree with one you already have).

An example of this: arranging things on your desk. I have seen people arrange items on their desk at work specifically for themselves to look at, which then forms a desired self-perception.

Is it possible that self-perception is more important than other's perception of you? Meaning, how a person perceives him or herself is more important than the actual perception, i.e., how others see them, i.e., the actual, undistorted perception. Or that a person forms a self-perception through the eyes of others, or as how a person *thinks* they are being perceived through the eyes of others.

When a person creates a perception, for example as a star athlete, the self-perception could be more important to that person than the perception that others have of that person.

An Example of Self-Perception:

1. I won't write back (an email) to someone who has horrendous grammar.
2. Subsequent self-perception: "I perceive myself not writing the person back. (Therefore,) I am not writing back to this person because I do not like (the someone)" … when, in fact, you may like them very much, but *can't stand* to read their writing.

Absolute Importance of Developing a Sense of Self

Fostered by parents.

The healthy development of a sense of self is vital to the development of a healthy adult. A key developmental element of a child is the extent to which the child is, after the guidance stage, allowed to perform tasks on their own and thereby receive the behavioral feedback. As a powerful example, allow the child to succeed as well as fail. This can be tricky, as too much assistance, or in fact too little, can be detrimental.

An absolute manifestation in young adulthood and full maturity is the extent to which the individual becomes an "active" agent as opposed to a "passive" one, i.e., the extent to which they will take the necessary actions to control the direction of their lives as opposed to simply letting things happen to them. As an example, take someone who is a computer engineer, and he/she works with operating systems but has a strong desire to work in the internet space. The extent to which that person will take action, or be an active agent, and do what is necessary to move into an internet-related position, as opposed to passively remaining in his/her current position in operating systems until the next managerial or otherwise decision or force acts upon them and causes their next career change, reflects their positive sense of self.

The phenomenon of the lack of sense of self is quite prevalent in a developed society if not the world. With catalysts such as crowd phenomenon, huge cities and countries, large corporations, parents who are simply too busy and/or too tired after a day of work to focus extensively on a particular child, etc., cause people's self-images to risk being completed in a healthy form, let alone initially placed on a healthy path.

Even the sense of self has a strong component of being environmentally determined. For example, I have a minimal sense of self in a few situations, but in writing I seem to have a strong sense of self. The image of my emails is very well crafted and painstakingly achieved, indicating a high self-image. Also, I see it in the fact that in signing my name (as "Mike") at the end of more emails percentagewise than most people.

Developing internal motivation versus motivation to please others is a key result of a well-developed sense of self. As a key example: instead of being a good person for the intrinsic value, you are a good person so you please your parent, so you get his/her approval, so you can feel good about yourself. Also, difficulty making decisions for oneself; what do you want versus what do they want you to do, is another reflection of a person's sense of self.

Work as a Function of Sense of Self and the Resulting Self-Perception of Its Positive Effect

Work is a mechanism through which a person builds an identity, expresses their sense of self, and confirms their existence. It is therefore possible for a person to overvalue his or her work, to add value and meaning when in fact it is present only to a limited extent.

An example would be a stockbroker who starts the new year out by making several trades in order to reaffirm his sense of self at a logical juncture, that being the new year. Though historically, his trades have flowed with market conditions more than his skill, and he will claim to have made "good trades."

The opposite effect can occur as well. A person with a low self-image can still strive to project a sense of self, but will, in the case of work, see fault and imperfection in their work, like an artist not liking his/her work.

The drive for attention, no matter if gained by positive or negative means, can also be seen as a means of affirming a person's sense of self. Entertainers, who emphatically promote their name, can fall into this category.

A person's "self-image" is directly tied to their sense of self.

A self-perception example: have a person buy a really nice, new car; will that person's self-image increase? As a person with a good, high, healthy self-image would buy a nice car, would someone with a defeated self-image, upon the purchase of a nice new car, due to self-perception of "their self now being high-end" experience a permanently elevated rise in self-image?

It can also be seen that the lack of expression of oneself is an expression of oneself, in that it communicates or expresses a lack of self.

Enhancement of and Protection of Sense of Self

Anything that either gives you a more positive or negative sense of self is powerful. For example, if someone compliments you on a posting to social media, you will then probably be more likely to go on that site. You will value the site more because that is where the posting is that valued yourself.

Conversely, the core of all core feelings is "I am bad." This is identical to having a negative image of yourself and shows, by its "coreness," just how essential your sense of self is.

Exist [Note: keep this with "Sense of Self" above]

"I think, therefore I am**.**"

To prove one's own existence [to oneself.] I think, therefore I exist.

Do I Exist?

The most abstract element of my thinking in this work is centered around an individual's drive to "confirm their existence." It maintains that the effort of an individual to establish and confirm his/her own existence is a central drive of his/her existence.

This drive can be seen in many of the individual's behaviors. The general category of behaviors designed to attract attention to themselves serve to confirm to the individual that they in fact exist. Behaviors such as making "unnecessary" noises, such as the tapping of fingers on a desk, unnecessary, fidgety movements, playing "peek-a-boo" as a young child with a parent, and compulsive talking, all establish to the individual the belief that they exist. The constant talker, in fact, is proving to others that they exist, and through the perception of others, they create the self-perception of same. Or those wonderful people who start talking *right* when the movie starts because they know your attention becomes focused and they can yank it onto themselves.

Positive behaviors such as creating fine art, acting in the performing arts, and playing and singing music all confirm to the individual that they in fact exist. Writing, any endeavor that has as an attribute the placing of the individual's name on it, even as simple as signing an email or even sending an email that will have the individual's email show up in the receiver's inbox with his/her name on it, is reinforcing to the individual his or her existence.

Our work is a primary means of confirming our existence. Many times, we define ourselves through it, we *closely* identify ourselves with it, and sometimes we become overly obsessed with it. Because of the role it plays in solidifying and materializing our existence. This is evolutionarily advantageous in that someone who works hard and provides for him/herself is more likely to survive. I see this behavior primarily as being learned throughout the lifetime of the individual and therefore of advantage to them in their life. A productive worker is also more likely to marry and support children, who will then be taught and therefore learn the value of work.

Unfortunately, if an individual's sense of existence is not met in a healthy manner, they can resort to negative behaviors, which have been learned to provide them with that sense of existence and sense of self. Behaviors such as vandalism, violent acts, or threats against other individuals, which are visible to both others and ultimately the individual himself or herself, establish and confirm their existence.

An extreme case would be when someone with a component of a very negative self-image actually goes to the length of creating a negative external effect, such as being very annoying. Not only does this achieve the goal of affirming an individual's existence but it creates a negative perception and therefore a negative self-perception, which is congruent with their internal negative self-image. Perceptions most always match feelings, with causality flowing in either direction.

It is often said that an exaggerated, developed "ego," in the vernacular, is developed to counteract a sense of smallness. While debatable, if true in many, if not most situations, this sense of smallness is closely equivalent not to having a well-established sense of the individual's own existence.

Closely tied to the concept of an individual establishing a sense of self-existence is the sense of self itself. The healthy development of a sense of self has been written about extensively and plays a prominent role in psychological and therapeutic theory. The individual needs an assured sense of their own existence to attain a well-developed sense of self. And conversely, needs a healthy sense of self to confirm their existence.

Itch

I've often said to myself, (half-seriously), that if I ever write a book, the one idea that I want to get across is what I believe to be the purpose of the "itch." I believe it to be, in some cases, intrinsically related to body language.

Some forms of an itch are an extension of the furthest reaches of the nervous system, to the skin. The nervous system, as we know, is connected to, or more properly said, originates from the brain, and mind, which are, among other things, the master controllers of the human body.

It is my theory that an itch in a particular part of the body has as its first, or first several, occurrences as a strictly biological event, i.e., caused by a skin phenomenon, or perhaps by an insect bite, etc. At some point, however, the mind "learns" the particular body movement, or body language, that is produced by the scratching of the itch.

At that point on, the mind, or brain, "produces" the itch, through the nervous system that it controls, in order to produce a specific body movement, or body language.

I believe that body language is a powerful means of communication between people and can be broken down and interpreted scientifically.

I also believe that communication between people, either with words or non-verbal, is extremely important as we are completely and thoroughly a social being. Many body movements, I believe, are in fact partially or fully forms of communication.

I need to state, however, that as powerful as it is, I believe that the communication that occurs in body language, more formally known as a form of non-verbal communication, pales when compared to verbal or written communication. To say that body language is more significant than verbal or written communication makes a mockery of thousands of years of cultural evolution of language, of the handing down of knowledge, both verbally and through writing. Our languages and their brilliant uses are one of the most significant attributes that distinguish us from animals.

Manic Stories

"Programmed Economy"

> In Trailer
>
> Brain Salad Surgery Full Blast
>
> All the Lights On
>
> Electric Typewriter – "Random" Typing
>
>> Emerson/Bowie Dancing Light Figure in Mirror
>>
>> Produced Three-Page "Paper"
>>
>>> Three-page Paper Shown to Professor Bach, on President Ford's Council of Economic Advisors
>>>
>>> Fed in Paper into TV Screen at Alpha Delts

The Trip in the Trailer

> Four Albums: 2 Beatles, 2 Yes. Playoffs.
>
> George Washington Head of Light Rising up through Tube of White Light
>
> On Top of Hoover Tower: Daryl Taking All the Jews to the Moon
>
> Snakes on Parking Lot of Medical Center (symbolic of medicine shield)

Thanksgiving '77

> Drove MGB through "wooden horse" – shattered windshield
>
>> Stopped there and cleaned out car in park
>
> Then, Drove through New England
>
>> Kept Nodding off on Highway – Kept Bouncing off Concrete Median
>
> Tried to Sell an Ounce of Gold in Harvard Square (no buyers in 70's)
>
> Had no Cash – Busted for Running a Gas Station

How Messed-Up High School Education Currently Is

Today's high school students are driven to get into elite schools. Driven insane.

This is evidenced by the sharp increase in the number of applications to elite schools in the last few decades.

College offers a tremendous experience. Elite schools do (probably) offer the best experience, especially Stanford, but R.U. offered a great experience, too. However, it comes down to:

1. What you do to get in, and
2. What you sacrifice.

To get into an elite school, do you sacrifice your physical and emotional health? Sleep?

The point is, getting into a great, or a good, school, and/or achieving a great or a good degree of success is a valuable, honest, and (at times very) rewarding endeavor. Having a degree from an elite school can be life-changing in a very positive way and an accomplishment to take with you forever. It is all a question of balance and sacrifice. The higher you go in life, the more sacrificing is justified. However, in a rational sense, there is no justification for a ruined life.

Sometimes, it appears all the student knows how to do is get A's. They are not trained nor prepared for the demands of living a practical life. This is in no way to say that bright students are deficient when compared to lesser-achieving students; rather the emphasis on grades has detrimental effects across the spectrum of all students.

Building "Resumes" in H.S.

The first time I heard the word "resume" used in a high school context, I was shocked.

The first time I heard the word "semester" used for high school, I was also shocked.

And "midterms" and "finals" in high school?? They didn't have these when I was there.

The goal of making high school more like college regimentation and a job search is like abandoning child labor laws and forcing children to take on adult work.

More and more homework 'till 11:00

Eight activities

Summer academic camps (this is the one I can't believe)

- Whatever happened to going to summer camp and playing basketball, softball, and going to socials? Don't you feel sorry for kids going to math camp *in the summer*?
- I won't even mention the SAT classes….

The number of standardized tests today's students are met with is absurd. It starts with grammar school. It has increased substantially over the past few decades and shows no signs of letting up.

Playing a sport to win for the reason of winning/get a good time rather than how it will help you gain admission into college. Is just plain sad.

Start to develop intellectual freedom, or at least *intellectual curiosity*, for example, taking an elective such as psychology, rather than taking a class because it is Honors/AP to build the college application.

In middle school, one marking period, my daughter had all A's and one B: an 89 (or 88). It was not good enough. She made honor roll. She was upset because she did not make high honor roll. In her high school, they only give out high honor roll (meaning they only acknowledge straight A's).

There is no doubt, however, that the young person/student internalizes the drive toward excellence. He or she takes on a will/drive of their own. This is a combination of initial parental push, which then leads into reinforcement by the school system, teachers, and exam feedback, and surprisingly, to a large extent these days, from peers. This internalization of a drive for achievement can be healthy, if not taken to extreme, as unfortunately is often the case given our current system.

Math is overemphasized, possibly at every level of education. I say this as one whose math skills were greater than any single reason for being admitted into Stanford. There is no doubt that a very high skill and dexterity in math is needed by those who move on to the science, technology, engineering, and math-related careers. But there should be some method to give math skills to these people without having to force four years of required math on everyone in high school, and in some cases, in college majors. The requirement for math education results in more students receiving it than is necessary. Perhaps only offer the latter part of the math curriculum when the student begins to form an idea of what he or she wants to do (this would "catch" a lot of "possible" STEM students) and continue into early college for more advanced math study. This would then form the math background that is necessary for higher-level college classes.

Sometimes I believe the reason why parents want their children to attend elite schools is so they can sit around a dinner party and say, "My child goes to Staaaanford." However, this awareness should not affect nor deter someone from attempting to gain acceptance into an elite school, or for that matter, the best schools he or she can get into.

I just realized the most amazing thing. When my child was in early eighth grade, still in middle school, I received a letter in the mail from her school. It concerned a program at Johns Hopkins called "Johns Hopkins Center for Talented Youth." The program was centered around providing exceptional students the opportunity for more rigorous study.

What amazed me was the following:

- That she had been *admitted* to *apply* to be *admitted* to this program.
- That she would have to take the SAT or equivalent, and score at or above the required level, to be admitted to the program.
- That this was for admission to a program at an elite school.
- And most of all, that this had happened to her when she was 13 years old.

SAT's in eighth grade?!?

Subjects that should be taught in H.S.:

- How to navigate life
- Cultural anthropology

Gives you an excellent perspective on other cultures, so you understand them much better as adults, rather than develop biases against them because they are different.

Also gives you an excellent perspective on *our* culture.

- Personal finance (investing, insurance, etc.)

A reason why people with degrees from the finest schools tend to, statistically, be much more successful than those without them goes beyond the school itself. Granted, the name of the school has enormous impact on a person's future. However, what must be *strongly* taken into account is the *amount of work* that was done in order to be accepted into the elite school to begin with.

Also, obviously, a person's intelligence plays a major role in the level of success attained. Contrary to popular belief, however, I believe that a person's intelligence is much more a product of the *amount of work* they put in, mostly all in school, by doing homework, etc.

The point I'm trying to make is that it is hard work and motivation that gets a person into one of the finest schools, *and that same <u>personal work ethic</u> gets them ahead in life.* Seen a slightly different but equal way, it is very hard work that builds superior intelligence, which opens the door to the finer schools and subsequently, success in their career.

Is it possible that one of the causes of school shootings is the intense academic (and otherwise) pressure the students are under? Also, possibly one of the causes in the rise of teen suicides?

To be fair, though, it must be said that students who graduate from these "modern" high schools, and most importantly have put in the time and effort, come out articulate and well-educated. They are well-prepared for their next step into higher education and to eventually assume the adult role of progressing us into an even better future.

Do I have a "rejection" complex about education? Did I form a negative attitude toward school because of deep-seated, education-related feelings of failure? In other words, I was "rejected" by the education institution via my not getting my Stanford degree, so I formed a resultant negative attitude toward academia. Or do I clearly see many misgivings, some of them quite serious, about the institution of education in our society? I still see Stanford in a very positive light. Also, I did receive a degree from a very fine school, Rutgers, in a very difficult major, Computer Science, receiving As in the most difficult classes with outstanding projects (having successfully built a compiler, an operating system, and a syntax-directed editor). And I was voted into the National Honor Society for Computer Science. But in all honesty, I do carry the remnants of the Stanford experience as evidenced by this manuscript.

It can be said that there is a strong contradiction in this book between my remorse about not having obtained my degree from what is categorized as an elite school, and my criticism of the current pursuit of elite schools in our secondary school system.

The differentiation lies in the demands made on our students in order to do so.

My criticism is not with the students who choose to pursue the finest schools, but rather with how the educational system and society have evolved to greatly elevate their value, and greatly raise the sacrifice. Like the CEO who sacrifices decades of at least ten-hour days, and currently works seven-day, 75-hour weeks under tremendous stress, it is the student's values, desires and drive that determine their decision to pursue. What is important is being aware of and making a rational choice.

Marijuana

> 11 "Then God said, 'Let the earth bring forth grass, the herb *that* yields seed, *and* the fruit tree *that* yields fruit according to its kind, whose seed *is* in itself, on the earth'; and it was so. 12 And the earth brought forth grass, the herb *that* yields seed according to its kind, and the tree *that* yields fruit, whose seed *is* in itself according to its kind. And God saw that *it was* good. (Genesis I:11-12)

My ultimate statement on marijuana is that it is state-specific. Meaning, you have to be under the influence to make rational, accurate judgements about its more significant effects.

What about the monetization of pot when looking at the legalization of marijuana as foremost a source of taxation revenue? Most anything can be monetized. In court, non-financial suffering inflicted by the defendant may result in a financial reward to the plaintiff. However, the monetization, or in this case, the viewing of the legalization of marijuana primarily as being tax-producing completely reduces, if not ignores, the marijuana-induced experience as well as other benefits.

Also, comparing marijuana to alcohol is like comparing a rabbit to a cow. They both have four legs. Even a rabbit stands on two legs.

The days when I would walk into a room full of people and put my head on a bong… It's amazing I'm still alive. Without it.

Why are they so afraid of pot? There is an overabundance of scientific, medical evidence that pot assists greatly with many medical illnesses. It is a known fact that a certain strain of marijuana greatly helps children with an enormous seizure condition. It has been written that children who suffer hundreds of seizures a day have, with the introduction of medical marijuana, had their frequency of seizures reduced to the single digits per day. Yet most all states, as of this writing, 3/8/2018, have not placed seizures on the list of illnesses.

Families have been uprooted from neighborhoods and friends, let alone schools and communities, so they could move to the few states that have legalized such that marijuana is available to treat their child's condition.

Parallels Between Political Dissidents and Marijuana Users

Political dissidents and marijuana users are prosecuted and jailed. Link: both are seen as being radical, counter-culture Threats to the State. This could very well be a major reason why drugs are so heavily prosecuted in this (and other) countries.

Marijuana was closely associated with the counter-culture movement of the late 60's, shortly after which marijuana was not only made illegal, but classified as a severely dangerous drug, the same as heroin, which is absurd. This classification prevents research to be done on it, which conveniently creates a catch-22 in that, without research, legalization on a national level is being held up. Also, in all fairness, marijuana was a huge unknown to the "establishment," as it produced altered states of consciousness that they did not experience nor understand. This added to their fear of it, and therefore encouraged it to be (legally) distanced from mainstream society.

Two huge rushes when I smoked pot for the first time in six-plus years (December 1983):

1. Throughout our cultural evolution, we have recreated parts of our body in our engineering. We, and animals, have four appendages: we built a car with four wheels. Animals and people have two eyes: we build a car with two headlamps. We build towers. Now we have reached the final frontier: we build our minds into AI.
2. "We are in the midst of a Renaissance." Renaissance is defined as a flourishing of culture; especially as exemplified by the peak in music in the late 60's/early mid 70's, as well as the technological explosion of more recent years.

The horrendous, absurd effects of "testing" marijuana in front of someone with a white coat in an uncomfortable, unconducive setting.

One more use for pot: if your situation/level of achievement is much higher than your current view of it, pot will help you "realize" it.

Why do athletes, rock stars, etc., use marijuana? Not only to "recapture" the consciousness of the momentary situation/achievement, but to *realize* it.

Conclusion: the achievement never goes away.

Pot makes me at least much more intelligent.

The late teens show awkwardness because it is a peak time for social development, and that since the late teens is a common time to start smoking pot, and possibly a time to smoke more of it relative to most other times in a person's life, it may appear that pot causes issues with social development, when in fact it only correlates with no causal effect. In fact, with me, I say that smoking pot "turned me social" in my freshman dorm.

Did the pot cause permanent damage? They say the brain is still developing in the teens and smoking a lot of pot during the developing years can be very harmful. I *did* do well at R.U. in computer science, etc., classes (put in three big projects), then after round two (1984-87 pot), I did well at AT&T, crossing that impermeable barrier from the business units to become an employee in Bell Labs.

It is said that marijuana use precedes the advent of bipolar disorder. However, a common age to begin the smoking of marijuana is around 15 (though there is obviously a wide range). The known common age of onset of bipolar disorder is about 19. Therefore, statistically, pot use will precede bipolar disorder yet not necessarily cause it.

There is no doubt that marijuana smoking can result in addiction and/or mania. Based on much reading on the subject, it appears that it will possibly cause mania in those people that have a predisposition to it. It can trigger it, as can many life events such as the first real job, a serious relationship, or a powerfully adverse event. However, there are simply way too many people who smoke it on a regular basis, and not only do they not develop manic symptoms, but go on to lead very successful lives.

Interesting concept: correlation versus causality, especially with pot.

Theorem: people who by "nature" are curious enough to look inside and outside of society's bounds, "to experiment." Some people just don't want to exist within the bounds of society. People outside of society would often question core institutions, values such as education, government, business, religion. Many times when they are already outside, they seek out or at least are a lot more casual about or *are curious about* pot, because of all the positive, wondrous, (bay-area peace-love-60's type cultural things, colors/art/music), and also because the reasons – negative incentives – such as "falling off society's track" are already diminished.

This makes it appear that pot usage "caused" people to "leave society," when in fact they already had.

Be careful with it. You can end up horizontal on the sofa. Or you might think that you have it too good.

Intelligent Thoughts

High energy linked to survival drives/behaviors. The energy produced serves to supply energy to fulfill the need. The stronger the need, the stronger the energy to fulfill it.

Examples: hunger, sex drive, fight or flight, drive for money.

Also, anything learned/associated with any of the above will be learned "strongly" and quickly due to the high energy.

Cognitive dissonance can be seen as an energizing state where the energy is used to resolve the dissonance.

Behaviors selected for either survival or procreation should ideally match. I.e., a behavior that selects someone for survival should also select that person for procreation. For example, a person who has achieved wealth is not only more likely to survive due to his/her ability to provide for their subsistence, but also will be more likely to be chosen as a partner for procreation due to their ability to provide for his/her offspring.

Precognition

I am absolutely certain, beyond a shadow of a doubt, that precognition exists.

After thousands of distinct experiences, probability or other explanations don't seem to hold up. Except for one key experiment, they simply haven't figured out a way to prove it in the lab. (There is discussion in the scientific community these days about issues in reproducing results from experiments, in certain cases, due to very large datasets and differing methods of interpreting the data. This is certainly not to say that science is invalid, just that scientific method has yet to be perfected when presented with new technological tools that undoubtedly will prove to be very valuable.)

Two properties of a precognitive event that I can see:

1. There seems to be an *"energy pop."*

This would be extremely evolutionarily advantageous. For example, in the animal world, if a bird were to be able to sense a predator coming around the corner before the bird reached the corner, the bird would have the opportunity to prepare itself and fly away at the moment of the sight of the predator. Note what I mean by "energy pop": the sighting of the predator produces a high degree of energy to the bird, which somehow produces the precognition. Perhaps in the lab they should test for precognition using high-energy-producing stimuli.

Note that, in this example, the stimulus/perception would still have to be experienced, i.e., the bird would still have to sense or see the predator. If the sight of the predator caused a precognition in the bird such that the bird was then able to immediately fly away before the predator appeared, this would present a paradox in that the bird never experienced the predator to cause the energy pop. This occurrence is similar to Stephen King's concept in the book/movie, *The Dead Zone*, where a negative event can be experienced, but then avoided as if it never happened. The "experience" of the predator would be a "dead zone," in that it happened, but in linear reality it did not.

2. The dream state is particularly susceptible to precognition.

What really surprised me here is that when I looked up precognition online, the topic of precognitive dreams was often written about. I have experienced many precognitive dreams and came to the conclusion that they were common (at least in me) before I read about the prevalence of reports of precognition showing up in dreams in other people.

(This is not to say that I had a "precognition" that I was going to read about precognition in the dream state, but merely to emphasize that for years I have been aware of the relationship between precognition and the dream state, only to see this confirmed in many reports.)

An interesting note: one of the articles said that psychiatry dismisses precognition as a delusion. Now I wonder, how many of my "delusions" are in fact not delusional at all?

Evolutionary Psychology – Boo

This section caused me to pause and think. Whenever I entertain a serious theory, either from an external or my own origin, I mull it over sometimes for years, taking in what I hope to be objective-as-can-be data, before I reach a conclusion. It is such that the thoughts behind a manuscript like this are constantly evolving, and therefore there never seems to be a right time to sit down and write it. All I can hope for is a coherent snapshot in time.

I have trouble believing that a good deal of our behaviors was selected for one million years ago.

I have often said to myself that all of our behaviors can be traced back to an individual's drive for survival. I realize now that I need to stick an "or" in there, and properly say "drive for survival or drive to propagate." (As an aside, I have wondered which of the two drives, individual survival or reproduction, is a greater drive. I believe individual survival because you have to survive to reproduce.)

I do accept the likelihood that some behaviors could be genetically encoded and therefore passed down. Fear of the dark, for example, is very real. It is easy to see how a prehistoric person would benefit, survival-wise, from having avoidance of the dark in that he would stay safer from predators.

If there's a gene for any behavior, if there's anything to evolutionary psychology, then there is a gene to defend ourselves. Perhaps that partially explains our strong emphasis on defense. A gene to defend ourselves physically, and also psychologically, to defend ourselves, our "selfs"; to become defensive.

What I believe to be genetically encoded, selected for, and therefore passed down, is the ability to learn. In other words, the development of the human brain as it currently exists as a biological organ.

It is true that there seems to be a correlation between what a parent does for a living, and the field the child enters. Doctors especially seem to produce doctors. Can it be said that there is a gene to practice medicine? To be an engineer? You *could* say that there is a gene on how to build a fire that would be the precursor to engineering. I don't see how someone who has no skills would be selected out because they would perish, such as by a predator or starvation. Perhaps they wouldn't be fed because they had no value to the tribe? I also don't see why a person who *could* build a fire would be selected for, how that skill would give him a reproductive advantage *on his own*. Perhaps he would be fed earlier. More likely, it could be seen on the social level, in that a tribe with members that possessed certain skills such as building fires and making tools and weapons would survive *on the tribal level*. And pass on those genes.

Evolutionary biology in modern-day context seems incomplete. It seems more likely that someone with the ability *to learn* would be able to learn the survival skills *of the day*. How could the ability to make horseshoes 250 years ago have a gene for a parallel behavior in prehistoric times? What is the precursor to microprocessor design? It seems much more plausible that the *potential* has been passed down genetically, but the skills have been learned *within the person's lifetime* because it fit in with the cultural survival *of the day*. Note in this context the word "survival" is not meant as in bare-bones survival, but in how a culture has built upon these basic needs over time.

Note how I do support the commonly held belief that behaviors have a genetic basis but are influenced by the environment.

As an interesting paradox, what if we are not born with the ability to learn, but are born with the ability to learn how to learn? This would still imply that we are born with an ability to learn. The point being that we must learn how to learn. Perhaps the educational system, particularly in the earlier grades should focus more on developing the ability to learn rather than just on learning itself.

Does behavior primarily evolve over time, through generations, or is it primarily learned within the lifetime of the individual? Or both?

I am of the belief that the majority of an individual's behavior is acquired, or learned, throughout his or her lifetime. People from previous generations teach, and possibly more importantly, provide examples through having their behaviors modeled. This provides a vehicle for behaviors, as well as attitudes and beliefs, to be transmitted through the generations. But each individual will *tend* to learn and retain behaviors that are only relevant to his or her lifetime. For example, the behavior of going to bed at sundown and rising at sunrise will not be transmitted or learned through the generations due to the advent of electric light (and previous fewer effective forms of interior lighting).

This emphasis on learning within the lifespan of an individual would explain the capability for rapid change in culture over time and gives hope that we can move toward a better world sooner rather than later.

Social Perspective on Natural Selection of Behavior and Traits

Let's step back a second on something I just said. In a sentence, *what if the selection of some behaviors and traits are best seen on the social level rather than the individual level?*

Humans are social beings and have always been so. In our entire evolution, our journey, we have existed in everything from tribes and societies. But never alone. A person would not survive completely alone at any point in our evolution except under extraordinary circumstances.

Going back to my example above, let's look at the person who knew how to make a fire. "Simply" being able to build a fire would most likely not afford that person an evolutionary advantage. The fundamental premise that I draw here is that that person would have spent very little time alone, if any. It is true that *if* the person found himself alone, he could light a fire that would ward off predators. It seems more likely that he would have just returned to the group.

The main points are that the ability to build a fire would have been very advantageous to the *group*. And that the *group* could have given him priority in feeding. (Did you ever hear the expression "higher up the food chain?) That this feeding would make his survival more likely and give him a better chance to reproduce. But most of all, *having this skill within the group would make it more likely that the* group *would survive and reproduce.* That *the group, not the individual, has been selected due to the traits of the individuals within the group that were beneficial to the survival of the group.*

So, it can be seen that from the perspective of the group, in a social animal, the individual traits that are beneficial to the survival of the group would cause the group to be selected. And therefore, for those individual traits to be propagated. Because the group was selected.

A powerful leader is selected for not only for how power helps the individual, but for how a powerful leader helps the group.

An extremely skilled and talented researcher/writer on a medical school faculty is individually valued for her contributions. But it could also be seen on the societal level that she is valued for the contributions she makes to society, that society becomes more valuable due to her contributions. And that that society would be "selected" for having that additional value.

It is the society's current state of cultural evolution which determines the needs for particular research subject material, and values it accordingly.

The same for someone who writes a computer operating system (the software program that controls a computer). The operating system is very valuable today, and certainly advances the culture. But that exact same operating system 500 years from now would be worthless because it would add no value to the culture and its current state of evolution. It would not make *the culture* anymore "valuable" nor selected, and hence the individual who wrote it would not be valued nor selected.

The Selection of the Behavior of Awarding Status

An important point is that *the social behavior of valuing certain behaviors through explicit actions* is of extreme evolutionary advantage to a group and society. This behavior may possibly have genetic roots. For example, the behavior of feeding the firestarter earlier in the food chain. For example, the modern-day behaviors of giving awards, titles, awarding honorary degrees, embellishing financial gain, and awarding status to those individuals who have made valuable contributions to society is a behavior in and of itself that is evolutionarily advantageous to society and *has been selected for*. The group/society is selected for having this behavior because by *awarding* evolutionarily advantageous behavior, these behaviors are encouraged and therefore sought after, modeled, and developed within the society, to society's gain.

The behavior, the capability of awarding status itself had to have been selected for. By placing a value on status, and awarding it to advantageous behaviors, people strive for status and therefore perform the behaviors associated with it which are advantageous to the group/society and therefore to the people in it.

The selected behavior of assigning status, of assigning value through status, is how groups/society selects behaviors and therefore survive and advance. Society selects advantageous behaviors by assigning them status and related awards. These behaviors should be seen primarily on the level of being advantageous to society as opposed to the individual. And therefore, advantageous to the members of society.

The theory of sociobiology attempts to explain social behavior as being genetically determined. It should be noted that the focus of the work was non-human animal behavior, though it was extended to humans.

My main difference between the above and sociobiology is that sociobiology presumes a *genetic* basis for social behavior, while I propose that the behaviors that society selects by placing value on them are fluid in that they change over time as society undergoes the process of cultural evolution.

Another difference I have is that these behaviors that are selected by the awarding of status are then subject to social learning by other members of society due to the value that has been placed on the behavior. The existence of the MVP award in football causes football players to learn how to be as excellent as they can be because one of their goals is winning the award. The award values good football playing. And the existence of the award encouraged the development of better football players; it selected this behavior.

A fundamental point of mine and perhaps major difference from sociobiology is that the behaviors selected by society by assigning value though status, awards, money, and honorary degrees are selected by society due to its value to *society* as opposed to the value to the *individual*. And that instead of primarily being selected for individual *survival* and *procreation* the behaviors are selected for *societal advancement*. For the benefit of the individuals in society.

Social Natural Selection

This behavior of awarding certain behaviors can be seen as a process of *social natural selection* in that behaviors that reward *society*, that add *value* to society, are selected for *by society*. The behavior of writing a great textbook, which is beneficial to society, is met with an award. A person who founds a company that produces great products which are beneficial to society, which adds value to a society is given wealth. A doctor who by his/her existence is making a great contribution to society is given a title which is high in status. These behaviors, writing a textbook, founding a company, becoming a doctor, have been *selected* by society through awards, wealth, and status.

A very significant mechanism that society uses when it awards certain behaviors, in order to propagate the behaviors is social learning. The members of society *model* (copy, imitate, emulate) *the behavior that has been awarded in order to achieve the award themselves*. This repetition of behavior causes the behavior to be selected or propagated over time.

Evolution is to biological natural selection of traits (survival, procreation) as

Cultural evolution is to social natural selection of behaviors (advancement).

Note that the behavior is selected, not the person.

It is important to note that the behaviors that society selects *change over time*. Sometimes rapidly. Writing a textbook may be rewarded over a long period but the subject matter changes quite a bit. The train industry was very rewarding in the mid-late 1800's but now it is the auto industry, first internal combustion, now also electric and hybrid. Magellan was a highly skilled navigator; that skill was highly rewarded at the time. The skill of writing software is currently *highly* rewarded, with no precedent 100 years ago.

This changing of what behaviors are selected over time is evidence of the dominance of cultural influences over genetics in the selection of behaviors.

You could argue that a well-paid software engineer will be more able to provide for a stable family unit due to his/her wealth, therefore have children and hence pass his/her genes on. And that genes have been selected throughout human history related to writing software, such as scientific and mathematical aptitude. But the assumption is that there are genes that are favorable to writing software that existed thousands if not millions of years ago, and that behaviors in the future have a basis in genes that exist today. This places a limit on what behaviors can arise in the future because they are bounded by our current gene pool and selected mutations.

Your assumption is that every single behavior at any point in the future has a genetic basis, not only in the modern day but one million years ago.

Do human behavior, creativity, and invention appear to be bounded? You could argue for a gene for creativity, the ability to create something *completely new,* but that is getting very general, very "low level," such as a gene for *learning,* as opposed to a genetic basis to create a specific thing or category of things. Someone *may* have the *genetically caused* genius to create PayPal, an amazing electric car, his own rocket ship, and the foresight to bore ultra-high-speed transportation tunnels as a large-scale evolution of the subway system that could also be used to deliver goods and packages. All four creations are rewarded and selected by the conditions of current day cultural evolution. Even the materials, science, and economic conditions are properties of our current state of cultural evolution.

The changing of selected behaviors over relatively short spans of time is evidence that social learning is a main mechanism for transmitting behaviors over time as opposed to genetic transmission. Genetic transmission is not nearly as alterable as social learning. As culture evolved and became more complex and advanced, it is possible that social learning became more and more significant than genetically determined behaviors.

An interesting question is, what is the exact mechanism by which society *changes* what it selects, i.e., what behaviors it rewards?

Society cannot currently afford to select certain rare social behaviors. We are not at that point yet in our cultural evolution. Our social programs are a positive way of society valuing and selecting people rather than hurting them. This is the sign of a civilized society, the one we live in today. However, in a positive light, curtailing certain social programs and thereby "encouraging" people to work not only is advantageous to society but also *increases the people's* value *to society*. By increasing their value to society, they will be selected for by society in the form of even better attitudes, wealth, and status. And therefore, ultimately very beneficial to them.

This is another good case for the importance of positive role models. When shown a successful person, with desirable possessions, who has been valued by society for his/her contributions, it will encourage people, especially youth, to follow those footsteps to attain those goals. A definite way out of many social ills is by convincing, teaching that value-creating behavior leads to favorable circumstances. Because ultimately, society rewards those who add value.

Education is a very key vehicle for adding value to oneself. That is why public education is such a vital element of our society and must be supported and be a focus of attention.

Instilling a strong work ethic is also hugely important. 99% of people that have become successful, that add significant value to our society, possess a strong work ethic. A strong work ethic and the value of education go hand and hand.

In conjunction with the drive to add value to society and reap the subsequent benefits, society needs to be shown that many people *already have value* who are presumed not to. It is amazing the quality of job I have observed people do who are not appreciated by society in general. By making society aware of the hard work and amount of accomplishment of people, and the value they add to society, it will raise the level of appreciation and lower negative emotions toward people.

Could the current inequality be related to the current rapid rate of change of cultural evolution in that we want the "leaders" to "move it, shake a leg" due to current opportunities to advance culture? Note that a very large disproportionate amount of the extremely wealthy are involved with technology which is not only currently a prime mover of cultural evolution but currently exploding? Also, note the extent to which our technology leaders have already *advanced* culture. I say the iPhone is a *good* thing.

Further supporting this possibility that a rapid rate of change of positive cultural evolution produces a larger than historically "normal" economic inequality is what was called the Gilded Age. The construction and utilization of the railroad is what drove the advent of the Gilded Age. Leland Stanford and Cornelius Vanderbilt were two of the very significant leaders of this era. In fact, Leland Stanford drove in the Golden Spike at Promontory, Utah on May 10, 1869, that completed the First Transcontinental Railroad. The railroad enabled the transportation of people and goods over distances never imagined before. This spurred enormous economic activity which was one of the key factors in the extreme societal advancement of the day. Both Leland Stanford and Cornelius Vanderbilt became extremely wealthy, creating a large economic inequality, as they created much wealth that played a key role in larger than historically normal societal advancement.

They both founded and endowed great universities.

Intelligence as the Highest Valued Trait in Society
It could be said that intelligence is the most valuable trait in modern day society. Therefore, intelligence would have to have as an attribute that it strongly lends itself to being modeled. So people adopt intelligent behavior, which is highly beneficial. Also, intelligence would have to be highly selected for.

Success has to be highly selected for, and modeled, for the same reasons. Behavior that is successful is by nature valuable to society. Successful people are awarded status. That is why status symbols are, for better or worse, attractive. In ancient tribes, ornaments that were attractive were given to those with high status. Possibly, the attraction of the ornaments facilitated modeling. Jewelry can perhaps be seen as a modern-day manifestation of this. Expensive clothing is usually attractive to the eye.

Could bipolar disorder be a selected trait?

Pleasure and Pain in Evolutionary Perspective
We are "wired" that things that bring us pleasure are good for us, and things that are painful are not. In other words, things that are favorable for our survival and procreation, things that offer an evolutionary advantage, give us pleasure. Things

that threaten our survival and procreation cause us pain. This is a basic premise of evolution and natural selection.

Fruit gives us pleasure. It is good for us. Eating rocks is painful. It is bad for us. We did behaviors that caused us pleasure. We avoided painful ones. By having "pleasure" linked to "fruit," we ate fruit and therefore survived. We were selected because we "liked" a survival-enhancing behavior. Because it gave us pleasure.

A bird species that has adopted a mating call that attracts a bird of the opposite gender will be selected over a species that doesn't. But only if the bird *likes* to do the mating call.

My point is that when studying behaviors that are selected for, it is important to note that the behavior, its end result, and/or its reward gives pleasure or pain. Work is oftentimes not pleasurable, but the reward, such as a nice lawn after laborious yard work, or money, is. Think of pleasure as a "target," as being "attractive," as something to be "approached," as opposed to pain, which has "repulsion" and "avoidance" as attributes.

The significance of the pleasure and pain perspective is also seen when it goes "haywire." For example, doing hard drugs can give great pleasure yet be harmful to survival. In fact, they can take precedence over evolutionarily advantageous behaviors. The fact that they can take precedence over advantageous behaviors shows that, in a way, pleasure and pain can be seen as being more significant a determinant of behavior than the survival, procreation, and advancement value of a behavior.

Pleasure and pain as goals also work on a societal level. A society can be seen to gravitate to a "more pleasurable state," i.e., one that is more pleasurable for its members in general. Society is ultimately a function of the people in it.

This could explain how a society adjusts what it values, i.e., how it changes what it selects for over time. It uses "societal pleasure" as a target, and adjusts itself accordingly, always moving toward a more pleasurable state. (Sometimes not directly but over long spans of time.) It is this more pleasurable state we call advancement. Which implies that an advanced society is intrinsically more pleasurable. And less painful.

Since a society of cooperation by all countries vs. aggression "feels better," i.e., brings great pleasure to its individual members as opposed to division, therefore, according to the logic of the societal pleasure principle, we will reach a state of world peace, "simply" because it is the most desirable, most pleasurable state for society.

Yet, as much as I uphold evolutionary theory, including its variant of cultural evolutionary theory, I believe that evolution and intelligent design are mutually compatible. It appears *to me* that evolution is "overlaid" by intelligent design, that there is a higher intelligence somewhere. Evolution, in spite of all its flaws such as disease, also seems too perfect. The color and texture of a flower petal. A woman's hair. Fruit. A perfect circle. Aesthetics itself. Our technology when it works perfectly. Possibly some evolutionary leaps were facilitated by divine intervention, such as tool use, and language? Like when the monolith appeared in "2001: A Space Odyssey."

Importance of the "Here and Now" as a Determinant of Thought, Emotion, and Behavior

In a way it may seem somewhat obvious, but I think it should be stated. Look around you. Imagine your *immediate* realm of perception, all you see, hear, sense, especially see, as one big "picture," one big "circle." I believe the extent that this "picture" has on your current thoughts and emotions is understated. A huge amount of your current state is determined by your *current perceptual field.*

This for me is another interpretation of the concept of how the "environment" affects your cognitive/emotive state. Environment here meaning the "current," the "now," environment. Certainly, your state is greatly affected by your past, your genetics, your overall psychological and biological state. But as much as these factors do greatly affect the way you currently think and feel, where you are and what you see need to be factored into the picture as well. (Curiously, when manic, it appears to me the "here and now" take on a larger proportion of significance. It could be due to the speeding up of my mind, and the subsequent "increasing" of my perceptions? Or maybe I just notice it more.)

Even hypomania can definitely be triggered by the perceptual field. Sometimes I have my morning coffee on the back deck overlooking a river. Granted, coffee, a biological stimulant, is involved, but on a beautiful day, with the beautiful temperature and beautiful view, I find myself much more likely to be drawn into a hypomanic state, or at least a state of "deep" thoughts. Of course, I might be pathologizing the state by calling it hypomanic in the first place.

The ramifications of the effect of the "here and now" are significant. There may be occasions where someone is in a state of distress, and rather than administer emergency medication or possibly take other measures such as making a panicky phone call, all the person needs to do is find a much more comfortable "environment," or "picture." In fact, possibly someone experiencing a (mild) panic attack might be aided as such. Or someone in an anger fit just needs to find a "mellowing environment."

This is why it is very important to create a nice, friendly environment conducive to therapy in a therapist's office. And how I wish that doctors would somehow reduce the "medical" in their treatment rooms toward something more comfortable. And the same with hospitals. Imagine an aesthetic doctor's treatment room. Wouldn't that feel a lot better? Imagine a more aesthetic world.

The basis of intelligence is association.

There is only one "NOW."
I'd like to invent a watch that only says one thing on it: "NOW."

Track

- County Mile junior year – 16 years old 4:27.8
- Half anchor, senior year, county relays, indoors 1:59.8
- Came back to anchor mile relay in 52.5
- Half leadoff Highland Park relays, junior year 1:59.8
- Conference outdoors freshman year, won, freshman class record 4:53.3
- 1st time trial, freshman year, cross-country, which I won; 1st competitive race ever; against many people, some who had run all summer
- Sophomore invitational, cross-country at Bernards, top 10 (7th)
- Sophomore, St. Joe's Montville relays (early in season, rainy), half 2:0X
- Sophomore, Montclair relays, anchored distance medley – medal
- Sophomore, Highland Park relays – (rainy) anchored distance medley – cut off by Carr coming off last turn – 2nd
- Junior year, outdoors: after 1st dual meet against Westfield, which didn't count, went undefeated
- Cross-country, senior year: 1) beat Riley, Ball up the last hill on their home course, first meet of season
- Cross-country, senior year: 2) next race, out-kicked Schcavage from

300 yards back of him when he had 150 yards to go.
- Indoors, senior year: opening dual meet versus Lawrenceville: Lavino Fieldhouse: won half: 2:03

The better the track/(competition?) the better I ran.

Example: at Lawrenceville

Example: anything at the Jersey City Armory

Recruited by Lawrenceville, Princeton

Technology

Is it possible, that, as we (humans) add artificial organs and implants, such as artificial hearts (which has been already attempted) and other replacements for organs that are near failure, and, on a parallel stream, as we create robots and humanoid machines, that, in the distant future, humans and machines will merge? And that, as humans are enhanced with artificial organs, such as ones to make them stronger or smarter?

And human/machines will be created, as in manufactured, not born?

On computer technology: What do you want it to do? How do you want it to do it? It's going to do it 1) because it can (it can/will do anything); 2) because there is a need (as evidenced by the fact that you want it to do something).

Believe it or not, people want to do business with you over the internet. For example, people want to buy tickets for your events over the internet. As an example, I have been trying to search the websites of the three largest classical music venues in my area. Classical music represents a pinnacle of our culture, and in my opinion, should be enormously supported. However, the websites of these three venues are horrible. I cannot browse for a concert of choice without immense effort, and much of the time the poorly written/constructed website does not let me search at all.

In this day and age, there is no excuse for a poor website. A business's portal to the outside world is their website. In many cases, a business conducts more commerce through its internet website than in person. Like software, a website should be thoroughly tested by someone with no prior exposure to it who is non-technical, i.e., a complete novice.

Interoperability of Technology

It is essential that technology be interoperable as much as possible. Technology must be viewed as an essential, core element not only of society but of the human race. There should be no choice but to have all technology that operates together operate seamlessly.

All electrically powered non-battery items can plug into the same wall outlet. All cable boxes and streaming utilities work with all new TVs because of the interoperability of HDMI cables on both the content end and the TV end.

Obviously individual products, such as word processors and editors, will have different feature sets. But the software, as well as most all the features, should work on all platforms. As a good example, it would be nice if a document type were not only readable but editable across editors.

Look at how smoothly and wonderfully software works together within the same manufacturer's ecosystem.

There certainly are many standards in place which do allow for interoperability. As one of many examples, it would not be possible to send and receive email without them. Most all common web browsers have at least basic functionality across most all common platforms. But more, and very well-written standards are needed, and they should be adhered to. Imagine *having the choice* to bookmark a web page on one device, and having it show up on another no matter what platform or browser.

Certain features are "vital." Just as on a car stereo, turning or pushing the left knob turns 95% of them on, and turning the knob clockwise raises the volume.

Certain browser features, for example, such as refreshing the page, bookmarking a page, accessing bookmarks, etc., etc., should be looked upon as being "core" operations and should be placed in a standard place across all browsers. Or close to it.

Not all size tires fit all cars. Not all headlights fit all cars. But specifications are available that allow any manufacturer to make a tire or headlight for any car. If there were only one tire size and type of tire, all manufacturers' tires would fit. If software companies only have one editor, and on one platform, which they often do, the editor should work seamlessly across all platforms. It should be the responsibility of the platform creator to publish an accurate application programming interface (API). Or move toward a "perfect world" where all target platforms share the same API.

Two Golden Quotes on Technology:
"The purpose of technology is to alleviate the burdens of our everyday existence."
"Technology is God's way of ushering us into the Kingdom of Heaven."

Biggest philosophical dilemma in human race (that I can see, greater than free will versus determinism) is yet to come: when death is cured, the choice between eternal life on earth/universe or entering the Kingdom of Heaven.

When the computer <u>knows</u>… For ex.: you walk into the kitchen, and the computer/drink maker knows what you want at that moment, and it's waiting on the table for you.

Five steps forward, and one step backward.

People speak of the pre-GPS age and the post-GPS age. Now with GPS, we wonder how we got anywhere without it. I wonder what technology is yet to come that will make us look back, define a "pre" and "post" age, and wonder how we survived without it.

Robots definitely seem to fit this description. Imagine an age when *all* manual labor is done for you, everything from weeding the garden bed to food shopping to doing the laundry to we can only imagine what. Our age will be looked back upon as "when they had to do manual labor."

However, it is my belief that, unlike how we look back upon culture as recently as 100 years ago, our age will be looked back upon in many ways as an advanced culture. We're definitely on both ends of the stick in terms of technological advancement and yet somewhat primitive in that we still contend with disease, poverty, and warfare, but the existence of microprocessors, our communications systems, air/space travel, architecture, our products and merchandise etc., do classify us as being advanced, possibly for the first time in human history. Since we are the first advanced culture, we have no mindset for looking back on a culture and calling it "advanced." Future cultures will not have this issue.

Our imagination is bounded by what we are aware of now, what exists in our reality, or what we can extrapolate out from it.

Top 10 Problems/Suggestions for the Internet (in My Opinion)
    1.   Having to set up an account at most every website.

2. So they can send you heaps and heaps of junk mail.

3. Pop-up windows, especially the kind that float down right where your eyes are going to go. This is like having a knife cut off the front half of the whites of your eyes.

    Don't you think we need something like "decency laws?"

4. Way too much advertising.

    I know this will not change, certainly not by me writing this. But somehow just by writing it, it gives me a release.

    Perhaps a volunteer opt-in usage-based "pay internet" where we could be charged a miniscule amount per website or webpage visit, or on a per-packet (unit of internet data transmission) basis to support the website, rather than ads.

5. Jumping web pages because ads are loading. Like cutting off the back half of the whites of your eyes.

6. Occasional slowness. Sometimes, because ads are loading. Have you noticed how advertising just grows and grows? For example, how many more minutes of a TV show these days are consumed by commercials compared to X years ago? Europeans cannot believe how many minutes of a show are devoted to ads when they view our TV. Advertising is taking over and ruining our culture. Can anybody help us?

7. When things don't work.

8. One of the stupidest things I have ever seen on the internet is targeted ads for a product that you have (just) bought.

9. Don't time out online account logins for a long time, i.e., when a person is logged into an account, don't make the window that appears and says, "Would you like to stay logged on?" show up unreasonably soon. And certainly, don't log the person off "behind his/her back," i.e., with no notification. Also, have the scrolling of a web page (as in no clicks but scrolling) "count" toward being logged on. For example, when I look at my bank statement online, I scroll up and down the page. This should "count," i.e., register, as being still logged on.

10. Can you please get rid of those stupid bots that pop up and *supposedly* you can ask them a question and get something vaguely resembling an answer? The concept is great, and someday we will have an

"intelligent bot" or whatever it will be called where we can ask it *anything* in any grammar, broken or not, in any language, and get the accurate answer. But until they can accurately tell you the answer to your basic question, they shouldn't be there because they are incredibly annoying.

We're approaching a point where many, many sites will be available by subscription only. Sort of like in the "old days" of magazines where you would subscribe to a few magazines a week/month. This is somewhat understandable in that content providers have costs, such as writers, computation equipment, IT staff to run the websites, etc.; plus, in most cases they need to make a profit.

Yet in the internet, having access to only a few chosen websites doesn't suffice. There are just way, way too many quality websites of interest, to which we wouldn't want access cut off. Especially with portals that present content from many different sites on the same page. Only being able to read a few of the articles would be counterproductive. A pay-as-you-go model might be a good suggestion. The better the website, the more visitors, the more income.

PayPal is brilliant and useful beyond comparison. Every time I purchase something from a website, when it comes time for the payment, I practically pray that they use PayPal. It saves the hideous time of having to fill in the same information over and over again, namely your name (2 fields), your shipping and billing address (4 fields), your credit card number, expiration date, and CVV number (1 field). I memorized my credit card number and it's still all *incredibly* inconvenient.

PayPal makes all this *incredibly* easy. With just a few clicks and a password, *all of the above* is taken care of for you. It populates your name, addresses, and takes care of all your credit card information.

Many people don't like to store their credit card information online for security reasons. But in some cases you must, such as for any recurring bill that is charged to your credit card, such as for a utility or for example Netflix or Spotify.

Unfortunately, credit cards change. Even if you use the same card for years, and keep the same account number, the expiration date changes every time the card expires, and you are issued a new card. This means you have to go to every single site and change your credit card information. And since credit card fraud is, unfortunately, fairly prevalent, your account is closed, and you are issued a new credit card with a whole new account number and expiration date every time it occurs. And yes, this means going to every site it is stored and changing it. Which is difficult if a company only charges you annually and you forget it's there.

With PayPal, if all sites used it, you would only have to update your credit card in *one* place! *One place.*

PayPal would have to go to extremes, if it doesn't already, and I bet they already do, to ensure the safety and security of storing your credit card information on their site. With strong encryption, etc.

There should only be one PayPal. There should only be one form of this type of electronic payment service. Having multiple ones is like having multiple currencies; it would defeat the purpose. Multiple electronic payment sites would necessitate having to update your information in multiple sites, which brings us back to square one.

Goodbye Forms

Along the ideas of pre-populating the purchasing fields on web pages, wouldn't it be great if many not only web pages but other electronic "pages" could be *very* easily electronically populated? In other words, you wouldn't have to type in, or fill in by pen, the same, same, same information over and over and over again.

I've thought for a long time, in fact, that forms lend themselves to computerization, that they can almost be seen as being only one step away. Both have "fields." A form has fixed fields that get filled in, and a database has fields, or sections of data or words, which can contain most any information.

There could be a database that contains a lot of relevant data about you. You could opt-in or opt-out, meaning you could choose to participate or not, meaning you could choose to have your data stored in the database.

The advantages are enormous. If and when every organization joins in, you will never have to fill out a form again. All that is needed is immense security on the database containing your information. And a "key," or one unique field: a word or a name. And a cell phone.

The system could use what is known as two-factor authentication. You would enter your "key" on the form; then the database would do a "lookup," find "your" record, i.e., the record containing your information. In "your" record, there would be a field for your cell phone. The database computer system would then text a number or code to your cell phone. You would then enter that number or code on the same form that you originally entered your unique key on. That way, the database knows it's you who is at the form because it correlated the cell phone number that *you* originally entered into your database record with *your cell phone* that *you* are holding.

At that point, all the fields in the form would automatically populate. The electronic form would "know" which fields it wants, of course, because it is the form and it knows what fields it has. In computer language, it would "pull" the relevant information from the database and populate the form.

You would opt-in and/or opt-out of whatever fields you choose to store in the database.

Now, think of the forms you get greeted with when you enter a doctor's office. Even your insurance card information could be stored in the database. This way it could be kept up to date in one place for all offices.

This would work exactly the same way as the manner above. Once, for all forms, or whatever electronic form they evolve into, you would enter your unique key and have the code texted to your phone. You would then enter the code on the form. Then, all the appropriate fields on the forms would be auto-populated.

There is a sensitivity to having medical information stored and accessible in a database. The doctor's office and associated health practitioners would be the only ones who would have access to the health information. This is enforced by having the database "locked" and only software that is *"certified"* will be able to access it. This property of "locking" the database and *"certification"* of the software that will access the database will extend to all electronic devices that will wish to auto-populate fields in that not only will it enforce that an electronic device will only access the appropriate information, but that no outside forces will be able to access any information at all.

The advantages of using such a system in medicine is enormous. If taken in an ambulance, the EMT's would have access to your current medications to make sure no unsafe interactions with medications-to-be-administered occur, substances that you are allergic to, your medical history, your primary care physician, and whatever else is needed for emergency health treatment. Another huge use of having medical information accessible by the medical field is that doctor's records will be accessible to other doctors. These records would be kept in the database in a uniform, logical way such that the information could be read easily and entered easily. And you wouldn't have to fill out those pesky forms at the doctor's offices.

Mark Zuckerberg just wanted everyone to make friends, and reconnect with old friends and family.

I bet Jeff Bezos takes no satisfaction in putting small companies out of business.

Four Cornerstones of Our Society - Government, Big Business, Education, Medicine

The paranoia and negative attitudes that undermine our society with respect to these four institutions are enormous. This is functional due to the "10 percent rule": focus on the negative 10 percent to get rid of it.

Phenomenon: when an "entity" is very large (like any of the four above) much less than half of it can be negative. This can make the entire entity appear negative.

Take for example our government, and the negative attitude many of us have toward it. Look at the beautiful parks they have provided us with, on the national, state, and local level. These parks had to be funded, created, and maintained. This may sound like a trivial example, but one that should not be taken for granted, and is illustrative, much as is our highway system, or our constitutional republic as a whole.

Look at big business. Where would we be without all the wonderful products that are designed, manufactured, and sold daily. Especially the big pharmaceutical companies, who take a lot of abuse these days. When someone is sick, and in a doctor's office, the medicine is certainly not turned away then.

One time when I was living on the west coast I was driving through Oregon. It was very dark; it was a very hard rain. I was out in the middle of nowhere. Then I noticed my gas gauge was on 'E.'

I looked up and there was a giant lit-up Exxon sign.

Religion sits in center of the four cornerstones.

As an aside, this "10 percent rule" can be extended to parents. With the *huge* amount of influence a parent has over a child, the absolutely enormous number of actions that were taken or not taken on behalf of the child, which affected the child, some of the actions were undoubtedly negative, wrong, a mistake. These mistakes may make up a small percentage of all the actions or non-actions of influence upon the child. But due to the sheer number of actions, many must have been mistakes.

And, following the same logic, if a parent over the course of the child's upbringing makes thousands of decisions and actions, then, mathematically speaking, the worst one or three or five must have been absolutely horrendous. Such is the math.

We should keep in mind that many times parents are not at fault; they are "agents" of society and the values in the current phase of cultural evolution.

The travesty is that we sometimes remember the bad moves over the great ones. And the real sadness is that we don't usually realize this, and come to grips with it, until it is too late.

Is this a book of contradictions, or did I merely tell both sides of the story?

…Then I went back to Stanford and graduated. NOT.